D0908570

romancing the bicycle

THE FIVE SPOKES OF BALANCE™

ROMANCING THE BICYCLE

THE FIVE SPOKES OF BALANCE™

Written by Andrea Cagan

A JOHNNY G BOOK

THE CREATOR OF THE SPINNING® PROGRAM

JOHNNY G PUBLISHING, LOS ANGELES

Copyright © 2000 by Johnny G and Andrea Cagan.
All Rights Reserved. No part of this book may be reproduced in any manner whatsoever, except in the case of brief quotations embodied in critical articles and interviews, without written permission of the authors.

Spin®, Spinning®, Spinner®, and Johnny G Spinner® are registered trademarks of Mad Dogg Athletics, Inc.

For ordering information or permission to use material from this text, contact us on the Web at
http://www.spinning.com

Printed in the United States of America

Library of Congress Cataloging-in-Publication Data
Cagan, Andrea.
    Romancing the bicycle : the five spokes of balance / written by Andrea Cagan.
       p. cm.
    "A Johnny G book."
    ISBN 0-9703257-0-3 (alk. paper)
       1. G, Johnny. 2. Personal trainers—United States—Biography. 3. Cyclists—United States—Biography.
4. Stationary bicycles. 5. Self-actualization (Psychology) I. G, Johnny. II. Title.

GV428.7.C32 2000
613.7—dc21

          00-061761

FIRST EDITION
05 04 03 02 01 00   10 9 8 7 6 5 4 3 2 1

Production: Linda Jupiter, Jupiter Productions   Designer: Gopa Design & Illustration
Cover Image & Photos (except page 72): Stephanie Waisler. Page 72 photo courtesy of WBN/Enervit
Copy Editor: Sarito Carol Neiman   Proofreader: Henrietta Bensussen   Printer: McNaughton & Gunn, Inc.

I dedicate this book to God

For giving me the faith to show up,

To find a way to face the day,

In dark times, in lonely times, and all times

When I doubted I had the courage to coach

   and train my students,

Even when I thought I wouldn't live

   to see another day.

And to all my students across the world.

Thank you.

TABLE OF CONTENTS

JOHNNY'S NOTE

THIS PROJECT was an important task for me, a mentally irregular person having my fair share of head winds and hills to climb. And yet, I have always maintained that as a human being, my contribution to this life and to my students was meant to be far greater and more important than the stationary bike I built with my hands.

It has been my dream and desire to delve into a dialog that would last longer than a forty-minute Spinning class. My challenge to bring a book to life was initiated by a heartfelt student and very close friend who saw far beyond my limitations and weaknesses. It was our constant commitment, together, for five years that brought *Romancing the Bicycle* to fruition and allowed it to manifest as it appears today.

It is my wish that this presentation of insight and knowledge act as a beginning step for all of us, an invitation to take a walk, hand in hand, towards ourselves. May we all make and find some sense in the craziness that we endure every day, as we move forward and become more of who we truly are, in this adventure we call life.

Johnny G

My family and me.

ACKNOWLEDGMENTS

I WOULD LIKE TO THANK:

My mother, for saying, "Never look backwards, always go forwards."

Norman, for being my dad and showing me how to recover

My wife, Jodi, for being my heaven on earth

My daughter, Jordan, for being my angel

My son, Jason, for your loyalty

My daughter, Jackie, for your honesty

Leenie, for being Mom

Lou, for giving me your daughter

Toni, for being my blood sister

Paul, for being my friend and teaching me to listen to the guitar

John, for being my partner

Brad, for the beginning

Victoria, for being my sidekick

Stephanie, for being my student, friend, photographer and family

Lewie, for keeping the books in check, having no agenda
     and giving me an ear to bend

Melissa, for giving unconditional love to my children

Vannie and her grandmother in Brasil

Dr. Freeman, for being my shrink

And to Andrea, for having ultimate faith and confidence in me. During all your
many projects, thank you for taking the time to constantly show up and sit on
the couch in my house, tape recorder in hand. I especially thank you for being

there when I was so engrossed and obsessed, I didn't notice your eyes streaming or your nose running, and I didn't take the time to offer you a tissue.

Finally, I offer my heartfelt thanks to all of you who were there when I faced adversity, and to all of you who were not.

HIMALAYAN CLIMBER'S PRAYER

Ask yourself for one moment,
What have been your feelings
On the eve of some act involving courage?
Has it not felt something like this:

> "I cannot do this. This is too much for me.
> I shall ruin myself if I take this risk.
> I cannot take the leap, it's impossible."

And then supposing you have done this impossible thing.
Do you not feel afterwards that you possess yourself
In a sense that you never had before,
That there is more of you?

So it is throughout life . . . you know,
"Nothing ventured, nothing won" is true in every hour,
It is the fiber of every experience that signs itself
Into the memory.

—J. N. Figgis, Himalayan climber

Wire Man

THE PURSUIT OF HAPPINESS

IN 1998, I found out that life was not about the Spinning program, winning a race, riding my bicycle, or even the Five Spokes of Balance, a system I created. In the space of about ten days, my body stopped working, my mind went down and pure survival was in my face. I hit the ground running and my old tricks didn't work anymore. Life became so basic, it was about taking one breath — and then hopefully another. In those moments and throughout the many difficult months to follow, my life redefined itself in such a fundamental way, everything I thought I knew and all that I believed were challenged. It was the worst and the best time of my life, a period of great struggle when I discovered the truth about myself, my life, my goals and dreams, the love of my family and the importance of my relationships.

It actually began on the day that I was born with a serious chemical imbalance called "bipolar disorder." I suffered from it all of my life, but I never understood what was happening until it nearly killed me. I just knew that something was driving me to keep moving forward. I fasted too much, I trained too hard and I ignored my heart, all because I had no "off" switch.

The worst of the battle began on Yom Kippur in September of 1998, the Jewish day of atonement, when I fasted. Three days later, I realized it was time to start eating again but I was on a magazine tour that provided me with little personal time, besides the fact that I seemed to have lost my appetite. I managed to eat a little brown rice, I slept only a couple of hours a night and I watched the geometric patterns and lines that recently had begun flashing through my mind. I was so fascinated with these shapes and angles, I began playing martial arts scenarios all night long, planning combat techniques with multiple opponents. I forgot to sleep or eat. When I returned home, the geometric patterns increased and I launched headlong into a ten-day manic episode that nearly ended in my death.

My blindness to my condition was magnified by the fact that I never had felt better physically or mentally. I'd been training diligently for the previous six months and I was in the best shape ever. My body was light enough to do handstands with perfect balance and my mind felt astonishingly clear. I was performing martial arts exercises with physical dexterity the likes of which I had never even contemplated. I did one-handed cartwheels with great ease and I could jump up onto a ledge and pivot on one leg with no fear of falling.

My family was watching me during the days preceding the episode, aware that something was wrong but not knowing what it was or what to do about it. Finally, when Jodi watched me deliberately smash one of my guitars for no apparent reason, she knew I was in deep trouble. I moved on to bending all the knives in the house (I decided they were an unnecessary danger), smashing the windows and any other glass I could find, and then dumping flower pots, dirt and all, into the kitchen and throughout the rest of the house. I was losing my mind but I didn't know it, as I had a logical plan in my head that I was following. I just couldn't understand why other people, particularly my wife, didn't understand what I was doing. Why are they scared of me? I thought to myself as I stood on top of a friend's car, stabbing the only intact knife into the hood as he tried to drive away in reverse. Didn't they see that everything was fine?

I could go on to explain the disturbing chain of events that followed, but suffice it to say that I thought I was in a Shaolin temple, that I was a Samurai warrior, and that it was my job to bring the Buddha safely into Los Angeles. My mind was so desperately confused, I thought I was personally responsible for bridging the consciousness between East and West and for discovering electricity in the process. I sat on my front step beating my ceremonial drum, announcing to the neighbors (after I had barricaded the street off with the furniture from my house) that all was well. I couldn't understand why people walking their dogs were running inside until the police arrived to put an end to my delusions. I'm lucky I'm alive. It's to the police officers' credit that they didn't shoot the wild barefooted man drumming in the blue robe with the yellow moon and stars embroidered on it, the Gi karate pants with no shirt, and the topknot and long ponytail halfway down his back, as he performed a front karate kick from the top stair onto the ground, landing solidly in front of them.

Hours later, as I lay in the lock-up ward of the hospital with antipsychotic drugs pumping into my veins and no idea as to what had happened, life became simple. One breath, then the next, vomiting, passing out, an inability to walk, and finally the dark fuzzy place that was as close to death as I've ever been. At one point, I lost control of my facial muscles on the left side (the doctors said I had a stroke) and my ammonia levels skyrocketed, the toxicity blacking me out every so often. Without the help of my family, I still question whether I would have survived. During my recovery time, when I nearly collapsed from a twenty-minute walk with a cane, I wasn't even sure survival was what I wanted. How could I, formerly a superhero, fitness expert, inspirational speaker and ultradistance cycling champion *extraordinaire*, be reduced to this state of weakness and vulnerability? After I'd been spotted crawling along Wilshire Boulevard to get to the doctor, how could I begin to repair my ego, heal my body, refurbish my mind, regain my family's confidence and create a new life for myself?

This was a daunting task, the hardest challenge I ever faced and one that I work on to this day. During the course of my healing process—which included the diagnosis of bipolar disorder, drugs to return my brain and body to health, and therapy for my mind—I was grateful for each day that I awakened. Since then, after considerable research, I've discovered that there are an enormous number of people in the United States with similar mental disorders who are in desperate emotional straits with no idea what to do about it. Perhaps in some small way I can help.

I have slowly and methodically come to understand that I was born with a chemical imbalance that has created untold misery and devastation during the course of my life. I've also learned that my suffering, as well as my inability to stop it, was not my fault. It was a lack of the right chemicals in the brain that made it nearly impossible for me to hold a train of thought or to stabilize my moods enough to counteract depression and suicidal thoughts. I've spent far too much time frustrated, angry, feeling separate, uncomfortable in my own skin and unable to find positive solutions. Until recently, there was no place of peace for me. Even when I went to the ocean to relax, I could hear nothing but the jabbering voices in my own head.

Today, through the combination of the correct medications and powerful therapy, I understand why I displayed antisocial behaviors, why I wanted to stay home so much and why I talked incessantly. I was desperately trying to get people to listen to my pain and anxiety, to my shame concerning my learning disabilities and to my incessant struggles as I pushed as hard as I could to prove that I wasn't a dummy or an idiot. I wanted them to know (and I wanted to believe it myself) that I did not deserve to be discarded as a human being.

I know I am not alone in this quest. To some degree or other, too many of us fight the good fight and yet discover that the trophy at the end of the race cannot fill the emptiness created by an inability to feel our own hearts. I have learned that a state of fitness cannot exist in the body alone. You can push yourself physically, train hard, eat the right foods, get proper rest, and balance still may elude you. Without therapeutic support for your emotions, thoughts and feelings, as well as guidance to build a strong, functional nervous system, health and fitness will remain unreachable goals. Through the severity of the episode that nearly killed me, and the subsequent healing process, I have come away with some new pearls of wisdom. Please let me share them with you:

The present moment is all you have. You can put your life on hold while you train for the trophy, you can ignore your family and friends, make your body look and feel invincible while you convince yourself that you don't need anyone. You may even win the race. In the end, though, the trophy will not provide you with a warm shoulder on which to rest your head. It won't help you sleep or lead you into a place of peace. In an unexpected moment, any number of things can happen over which you have no control, things that can change the course of your life forever.

The truth is that we all have our demons and our battles to fight, so why not forget the future and focus on healing the past in order to make space for yourself in a satisfying present? In the end, the past cannot be cleared until you face each of your opponents, both physical and nonphysical, and take them down one by one until they are no longer opponents.

Finally, please remember this: I believe that healing your heart is not beyond your capability, no matter how far gone you may be. I also believe that peace is your birthright, that God and goodness reside in each of you, regardless of your thoughts and actions, whoever you are or whatever you have done. If you commit to living in the present moment and being the best human being possible, you can remove the obstacles to your heart and find that peace for yourself. Whether you are raising a family, pursuing an intellectual career, running a business or romancing the bicycle, peace and happiness are not only possible, they are just around the next bend, on the next page or in the next pedal stroke.

It is my heartfelt desire that my story might connect you to your own as you discover a way to access your courage in the unfolding of your life. It is up to you to promote health, happiness and peace within yourself, your family and friends. When you reflect on society and the world at large, you will see your part as a spoke in the wheel of life. Therefore, I implore you not to give up until you find a way to be happy, to accept yourself and to embrace the love that is waiting for you. Allow me to stand before you as living, breathing proof that no matter how bad it gets or how close to death you come, it can still be done. Allow me to remind you that it is a privilege and an honor to participate in this beautiful world we call our home.

Me at four and a half years of age

ROMANCING THE BICYCLE

THE SPIRIT OF SPINNING was born in South Africa when a dispirited four-and-a-half-year-old kid named Jonathan Goldberg climbed onto his first bicycle, pointed it toward the beach and started pedaling. This is where I found my spirit and my freedom, believing for the first time that there was a real place for me in my otherwise limited and disoriented world.

It was ironic that during apartheid, my first spiritual mentor would be our black gardener Shadrack, who lived in a shack in our backyard. I can still see him sitting in a cloud of smoke, a cigarette hanging out of the edge of his mouth, molding figurines from clay. Close by, a little white Jewish boy from a well-to-do family listens intently to this man's thoughts and philosophies. There, in Shadrack's room, the seed that now underlies the Spinning philosophy was planted and nurtured into a conceptual understanding: the constant shifting and changing of life, embodied in the words, "one pedal stroke to the next."

I marvel constantly at how this tiny nucleus grew into Spinning, a multi-faceted experience that expresses a wildness interlaced with an element of containment, elation in the midst of serious commitment, a sense of self-control mixed with speed and the illusion of flying. The thrill, the energy, the power and the sensuality that fill a room when I lead a training on my "Johnny G Spinner®" fills me with joy. With headphones and microphone in place, I face a group of beautiful, eager cyclists, all of us Spinning our legs to the music, dropping sweat on the floor and facing ourselves. What could be more exciting? I often marvel at how my romance with the bicycle produced the long-term marriage between structure and freedom that still motivates and impassions me to this day.

In the mid-eighties while I was I training for the Race Across America (RAAM), riding through long silences, unforgiving desert heat, freezing rain, with no money and little food, I developed powerful techniques and strategies — partly for survival, partly driven by my need to keep moving forward and not quit, no matter what happened. Out of this kind of training and focus came the Five Spokes of Balance, a system I created and utilized for guidance whenever the need arose.

The Spinning program, as it exists today in full maturity, emerged in the mid-eighties when I brought some stationary bicycles into my garage, along with a set of rollers. A precursor to indoor cycling, the rugged, violent sport of "Roller Racing" was prevalent in Europe and certain areas of the United States. During freezing winters, hard-core cyclists would drag a set of rollers into a bar. This piece of equipment looked like a treadmill about a foot and a half in width, with a speedometer, a distance gauge and three very slippery drums (two at the back, one in the front) with a band that linked the wheels. After swilling too many beers, the guys would place bets on who could go the farthest and fastest. Then they'd balance a bicycle on top of the rollers without support as each man took a turn jumping on the bike and pedaling as hard and as fast as he could. The idea was to stay upright and keep on rolling while the other guys shouted and drank in the background.

It takes absolute dedication and concentration to remain upright on the rollers on a good day. Just imagine these guys, rip-roaring drunk, furiously pedaling a bike that was sitting free and unattached to anything. The sound was fearsome as they went flying off the rollers, crashing into walls, completely wiping out. The next night, a little worse for the wear, they'd start all over again — until the weather changed and they could go back outdoors to ride. I actually trained my first students with the same kinds of rollers (minus the betting and drinking) along with any stationary bike I could get my hands on.

Based on my experience of riding rollers and being on the road for extended periods of time, I designed the first prototype of a Spinning bike. I went from training people in some of the most popular gyms in Los Angeles to teaching out of my house, working one-on-one with my rough, hand-welded prototype.

After extensively researching the stationary bikes already out there, I wanted mine to be something different: revolutionary, strikingly simple and easy to maintain. At the same time, I wanted it to offer everything a rider needed to recreate the experience of being out on the road. I had to find new locations on the bike for the chain and the resistance gear, so it was all trial and error as I instructed the mechanic to tighten something here, loosen something there. After several generations of prototypes, I had pretty much what I'd seen in my mind. In 1989 I opened my first commercial "Johnny G Spinning Center" in Santa Monica, California.

The first finished prototype had a retro look. The angle of the handle bars and the computer on the current stationary bike created a situation in which a rider could not stand up over the saddle. To remedy that, I gave my prototype a thick, beefy frame with a saddle that moved forward and backward, allowing proper seating angles and various positions for the handle bars so you could stand up and sit down at will. It was fashioned out of square tubing, a material that was available throughout the world. In order to make the Spinner® feel realistic, I added the option of real road pedals so a rider could clip on cycling shoes with cleats instead of ordinary tennis shoes, if he or she so desired. This meant changing the bottom pedal bracket and crane arms to handle a real cycling pedal. For decades, people had been riding flat platform pedals with a rubber strap across the foot. Not only did it easily come undone, it also forced a rider to wear tennis shoes instead of cycling shoes.

I painstakingly designed the prototype over an extended period, during which time I took on a partner, John Baudhuin. We created a company called Mad Dogg Athletics, and John and I took the bike on a four-year tour of the United States. Eventually we placed about five hundred bikes in major fitness centers in Los Angeles, New York and Texas, as well as in many celebrities' homes. After a lengthy and agonizing process, Schwinn licensed the bike from us, mass-manufactured it and began to distribute it. Schwinn's first "Johnny G Spinner" was painted white and introduced at the IIRSA Convention in 1995.

This was the turning point. The stationary bike would no longer exist solely for warming up or for burning calories before training. It would now be an entire workout unto itself, on a functional piece of equipment with real handlebars, a water-bottle cage and a variety of settings that offered the ability to emulate everything a cyclist did on the road — time trials, riding the flats, climbing a mountain, riding all-terrain, maneuvering bumps in the road, sprinting — in a single forty minute session. After so much isolation on the road, I envisioned Spinning to be something that members of a pack could do together while still maintaining their individuality. Most importantly, I didn't want it to cost a fortune for someone to participate in the Spinning program experience.

I fashioned the "Johnny G Spinner" and the training program in the spirit of a farmer planting a seed and making it grow. Rather than suggesting nobility of birth or lifestyle, my goal for the Spinning program was to inspire nobility of spirit. That comes from the inside out, so wherever I'm cycling at any given time—in my garage, in a gym or in a pack out on the road—that place becomes my training dojo, where we are all equal. It's just like the farmer working his field: noncompetitive, focused and dedicated to building character from a simple seed of desire.

As we arrive in the twenty-first century with so much technology, electricity and complicated machinery, so many lasers, batteries and cars, going back to what feels good and right can provide powerful insight. There is no technology that will guarantee us success. We are *already* successful, we were born that way. We have the right to enjoy the flowers, the rocks, the birds and the trees, to take care of each other, to be able to communicate truthfully and nonaggressively when we're angry and to work on ourselves with honesty and commitment. All we have to do is to change the way we think and manage our emotional states of mind in order to make the most out of what we have. Let's not wait until it's gone and then agonize over what we've lost. If we don't find peace or happiness, if our mind goes too far out of control, we may end up grieving a life that could have been rather than enjoying the one we are living now.

Statistics show that by the year 2010, gym memberships will have grown from about fifteen million to as high as twenty-five million. And still, Americans lead the world in obesity and in depression. The average American has a hard time living a balanced life. Our kids watch television instead of spending time outside. Many of us sit in front of computers far too long without taking the time to revitalize our energy and our states of mind. We make excuses for not taking the time to cook our food with real nutrition in mind. Stress-related illnesses are rampant. A huge percentage of people are overwhelmed and pressured, complaining that they just don't have enough time for their partners, their children, their passions and themselves. When we don't take responsibility for our lives, our bodies or our minds, we can end up with heart disease, lung problems and other degenerative illnesses. In short, we need to remain conscious, aware and alert in order to feel good and function in a way that will bring us satisfaction, rewards and inner peace.

Although the following pages reflect my personal story, I know you'll find some of the events universal enough to relate to your own experience. At the very least, they may provoke a good conversation. In the end, the reward is in sharing thoughts and ideas with someone, perhaps on a bicycle ride when the dialogue becomes so consuming that you look up ten hours later and you hardly know you were on the road. Marrying provocative conversation with the right intention creates the opportunity to become a majestic human being.

A final word: As I work to soften my own experience with life, perhaps your personal confrontation with adversity can become a little softer as well. Let's all strive to be brighter and more insightful as we develop an arsenal of tools to embrace our lives in a more loving way. The beauty of being human is having the ability to explore, to be dynamic, to be somewhat crazy, to get out there and do it, to transform and then to freely offer to others the unique pearls of wisdom we've gathered along the way.

In the spirit of joining together to make our goals and dreams come true, let's all get on the bicycle, turn the page and catch a ride.

See you on the road!

Race Across America — lonely roads of Kansas

THE RACE
ACROSS AMERICA, 1987

I JUST STARTED TO ZIGZAG along the road. That is, I *think* I did. My mind is playing tricks on me and I can't be sure what I've been doing for the last hundred
miles. In fact I'm not too sure of anything right now but the road in front of me,
because I can see it. I'm way in, thousands of miles in, riding on this bicycle, and
there's that van driving beside me. It's been there all these days, the whole time
in fact, and so has my crew, but I'm a little confused and I'm not exactly sure who
those people are. Or if they know who I am. There are times I wish they'd leave,
I don't feel safe with them, but the isolation'd be too terrible if they went away.
And somebody keeps handing me bottles of Evian water, so they'd better stay.

R ight pedal stroke, left pedal stroke, right pedal stroke, left pedal stroke.

When I first got on the bike, six days and more than two thousand miles
back (at least that's what they tell me but I'm not so sure), these same pedal
strokes were here but the road didn't look like this. It was Los Angeles, there were
mountains and valleys, brush and flowering trees, lush vegetation and houses by
the side of the road. My mind was fertile, I was hopeful, I had a clear goal and
I was going for it. But when I started, I wasn't in the shape I should've been. I
was physically underprepared, emotionally scattered, and my life was far from
being stable. I was also more chemically imbalanced than I could possibly have
imagined. To be perfectly honest, right before I left I was absolutely manic, staying up for days without sleeping and then lying for hours in a flotation tank,
thinking about nirvana and flexibility. I convinced myself that I could accomplish my goal no matter how I felt. I may have been nuts, but at least I was in
control of my breath.

Now, self-control is nowhere to be found; my breath has a mind of its own, it's just one heartbeat to the next. It's as if my breath is breathing itself, like I have nothing to do with it. Almost like I don't exist. My crew tells me I'm in Kansas. It must be true, there's nothing but straight road ahead of me and behind me, asphalt below, heat above. My skin is like a sieve; water leaks through it as fast as I can pour it down my throat. How long have I been doing this and how long will I keep doing it? Maybe forever. What time is it? Better still, what *is* time? Maybe this is hell and I'm riding a bicycle through it and it never ends. Maybe and maybe not.

Right pedal stroke, left pedal stroke, right pedal stroke.

Three thousand, one hundred miles. That's the distance of this RAAM, the Race Across America, start to finish. Los Angeles to New York City. For months, everything in me has been about that number, a magical distance to be courted, seduced, crossed and eventually conquered. The number repeated in my mind while I trained throughout the days and nights, in rain and snow, through muddy mountain trails and under the scorching desert sun with no people around and no relief in sight. Just me, the bicycle and a degree of physical pain that only comes when you've ridden for days on end: blisters on your rear end, quadriceps aching, eyelids drooping and nothing to relate to but a nagging, conflicted mind.

I think it must be like taking a birthing class and you think you have every-thing you need—until the labor pains kick in. Nothing could have prepared me for the spasms in my calves, the flesh ripping away from the seams of my cycling shorts on the back of my thighs and my butt, the sweat pouring down my arms like I'm a salty waterfall while parts of myself drop along the road, skin and sweat and brain cells falling away. It's my personal trail of breadcrumbs, like the ones Hansel and Gretel left behind them as they ventured farther into the dark-ness, hoping one day they'd find their way back. If I remember correctly, the bread crumbs were gone when they needed them. Hadn't the birds eaten them all? But at this moment I can't be sure I remember anything correctly.

The months of training that led up to this are like a dream. I vaguely remem-ber riding through sleeping towns in the middle of the night, passing dark houses with families warm in their beds and nobody to share my thoughts or reflect anything back to me. The bicycle was my metaphor and my mirror then, a pure and immediate reflection of my spiritual quest, my insatiability, my desires, weak-nesses and strengths. At times, it also reflected the emptiness that forced me to let it all go. From early on, the bicycle was my temple, my door to spirituality, since everything else in my childhood had been about abuse. But when I caught a ride on my bike, flying across the roads away from or toward whatever I pleased, I had a structure beneath me that I could hold onto, a sense of belonging and purpose that I needed more than food and shelter. The bicycle offered me fuel for my soul and structure for my body—two stabilizing forces in a child's chaotic world.

Left pedal, right pedal, left pedal, right. Oh dear Lord, if I lose my rhythm now, God only knows how I'll get this bicycle to my destination. New York City. It's strange to think that when I pedal the bike toward the city, it goes very slowly. But when I think of New York, I'm already there in my mind. Much more efficient than this painstaking pedaling. And the breathing. Even more than those pedal strokes, it's all about my breath. All the practicing, the planning, one breath and then the next, preparing for the big event. Hoping you're ready and knowing you're not. And then it comes; you keep reminding yourself to breathe but the pain is so huge, even breathing doesn't cut through it. And yet you keep doing it because it's all you have.

The idea is to make these pedal strokes disappear. Like I'm not even doing them. But they're all I have besides myself, the bicycle, my breath and my consciousness, which is questionable right now. And my hands, I see them gleaming with sweat, poised on the handle bars and I imagine that RAAM ring on my finger—the gold ring with a man riding a bicycle across a map of the United States. That'll make it all real and give it purpose. The question that's eating me up is this: Do I care anymore? Is a ring enough to keep me going?

If I could see into the future right now, I wouldn't believe what's coming. How can I even begin to imagine that in twelve years, this right pedal stroke and then the left will metamorphose into an indoor training method called Spinning —something I'm destined to create. I'll be a champion all right, but it won't look like I expected. Nothing ever does. The day will come when Jonathan Goldberg, that dyslexic, confused, raging kid without a clue as to how to make his way, will be a world champion called Johnny G, riding a stationary bike, going nowhere and yet accomplishing all his dreams and goals.

How can I begin to fathom this reality as I stare at the unending road ahead, deeper layers of skin on my legs tearing away, my sleep-deprived mind creating labyrinths of agony out of which there's no feasible escape? There's no way to see the future, no thoughts that can take me anywhere but to the next breath. Ah, the pain's back, my familiar old friend. The effects of the rubbing alcohol have worn off, my legs are beginning to burn again. This is good, I can feel myself. I'm here. I'm alive. Bump in the road. Beautiful bump. Momentary relief from the monotony—and now it's back.

There's Jack Scalia, a friend, waving at me. I trained Jack as a triathlete and he's way out in front of me on the road. Not on a bike though. He's not competing in the race. He's here for me, standing on his legs, flailing his arms around. I don't know what he's doing there, I only know he's motioning at me. I'm pointing this bicycle toward him and pedaling. Right, left, right, left.

I'm there. Jack's beaming at me but he's not allowed to touch me while I'm on the bike or I'll be disqualified. I feel like someone with a contagious disease, secluded in a bubble. Too hot to handle. He's talking to me. "Johnny," he's saying, "remember the cross I gave you before the race? The one you're wearing around your neck?"

I look down. There it is.

"Johnny." He's talking to me again. "Take the cross in your mind, turn it upside down and use it as a sword to cut through the pain and negativity."

I nod my head. It works for a few minutes—or a few hours, I can't tell the difference. But the cross isn't the only thing that's upside down. My mind is getting in the way. All I can see is the end of my bad marriage, losing everything, caring about nothing and no one, not even myself, troubled sleep, two hours at a time, four at most, dark depression, the searing pain of torn-up flesh, and people in the van who alternately look like demons and a well-meaning crew.

A fellow rider told me that once during the RAAM, after being on the road for a week, he started thinking his crew members were aliens who were trying to possess his body. He got so freaked out, he drove off the road and he wouldn't take any food because he thought they were trying to poison him. It's normal to distort reality after five or six days of sleep deprivation. You get into an altered state and you lose sight of what's real. I know this so it's not like I think my crew want to possess me. The truth is that I'm so far away, my mind is so conflicted and my heart is so broken, I can't relate to them at all. Except to take water from them and be careful of them. I'm not sure they mean well and I know I need them. A dilemma.

So why am I doing this? I forget. Better not ponder that one. "Why?" is a bad question, a dangerous tributary of thought to follow. That's because here in the middle of Kansas, there's no answer that will satisfy me. And yet I can't help asking. It's as if the thoughts are thinking me. Just like my breathing. I wonder if my consciousness is really mine. What am I without consciousness? A bunch of pedal strokes that aren't connected to anything. But there has to be a reason I'm here beside my desire to arrive at the finish line as one of the greatest ultradistance cyclists of all time. I want connection. So how come I've never felt more disconnected? Dirty trick, isn't it? I can hear myself laughing but I can't feel it. Maybe it's somebody else.

"Your heart rate is too low. Can you pick it up, Johnny? You're falling behind." It's my crew manager. His words cut me because they make no sense. I'm so all alone, why doesn't he encourage me? Can't he see that I'm going as fast as I can and I need some understanding? Some kindness. A little compassion, support and sensitivity. Some inspiration. The idea is to find a way to make these pedal strokes go away, like I'm not even on the bike at all. Right now, I can't seem to do it.

There's Jack again, a tiny benevolent figure up ahead, the sun rays behind his back lighting him up like an archangel as he motions for me to ride toward him. My legs are moving the bicycle in his direction, even though the saddle is wreaking havoc on my skin. The blood is staining my riding shorts but at least I have some structure beneath me. The only structure I've ever really known.

Before I knew myself at all, the bicycle was all I cared about. I was a lost kid. My childhood had bullied me along a narrow path of abuse and suffering in a world completely devoid of nurturing or structure. My father was a tremendous athlete, a champion squash player and a record-setting one-mile runner. I so desperately wanted his approval that I put aside my own trophies and kept his on my bedroom shelves, trying to win his attention. But it only added to my pain every morning when I opened my eyes to my father's accomplishments, plagued by the sense that I could never measure up. My two sisters, Susan and Lynn, and I watched him hold everything in, unless he was angry. Then he would let us know. I found his life to be sharp-edged and unforgiving, exclusive of any heart or soul.

That was before I knew him as a human being, before I could appreciate the beauty of the man and his pearls of wisdom as an athlete. His own dad died when he was nine and his mom remarried at least five times, maybe as many as seven. He was raised in a strict boarding school and apparently he suffered from depression. But he was stoic in his beliefs that as tough as it was, we all needed to face our lot in life.

He was the one who taught me things like:

When there's no time to stop and regain heartbeats, recover while you're in motion.

That's what he did when he played squash. Wise words, but as a kid, I didn't understand their value.

My mother was a loving woman, yet my father's energy and abilities so overpowered her in my mind I could hardly feel her presence. I remember how frenetic she was, thinking about ten things at once, keeping herself on the rivet most of the time by starving and drinking ten cups of coffee a day. Isn't it ironic that such a brilliant woman, with a photographic memory and the will and intelligence to put herself through university at the highest level, would die in her late fifties of Alzheimer's disease? She was anorexic and she had something they might have labeled manic-depression today, or, the more popular term, bipolar disorder. She went undiagnosed at the time; she died thinking she was losing her mind, with my father doing everything for her, from dressing her to doing her make-up, even though she had a full-time nurse.

I'll be finding out the hard way that I also have bipolar disorder, about twelve years from now in a dramatic emotional and physical crash. But not yet. Life plays tricks on us just like it's doing with me right now, creating hallucinations on the road, ghostly memories from my past, challenging me to face myself. I cower for a moment and then I pedal right through them, dissolving the abuse and ridicule of my childhood.

I grew up in a hopeless world—until I saw my first bicycle. It was my sister Lynn's, and one of my earliest memories is knocking her off that shiny new bike into a rosebush on her birthday because I wanted it for myself. In fact I'd never wanted anything so much. I finally got my own bicycle at four and a half years old, and it was instant love. I romanced it every day, meticulously cleaning the spokes and breathing in the smell of the oil and metal. I listened for the click of the gears, I savored the texture of the handlebars. For me, everything good and hopeful in the world existed on that bicycle, rolling down the street, listening to the sound of the tires. Add to that the opportunity to be out of metaphorical chains, a sense of independence that I could take this body and fly, to feel the burn in my muscles and to embrace it not through fear but through liberation.

Knowing I could point the bicycle somewhere and it would just take me, gave me my first sense of real connection. I melted into the soft finesse of the harmony between the machine and my body, as the rubber tires became my feet. I felt the symmetry, the balance, and I loved tasting my breath and feeling the headwind disappear.

There doesn't seem to be a headwind right now. Or any wind at all. I wish it would blow between me and the bicycle seat so the burning pain in my thighs and my butt would go away. Really, everything hurts, even my eyelids. At least the suffering lets me know I'm alive. When I started this race in Southern California an eon ago, anxiety and claustrophobia would arise momentarily and I could dissolve them. Clarity would come back and my consciousness would soar. Years of martial arts and Zen training came together in the most perfect way and I'd get through the emotion, letting it melt. One hour blended into the next.

That was then. Now I'm crawling in my skin, I'm so anxious my mind is careening out of control and all I can hear are the words, "I can't do it. I can't do one more pedal stroke. I need to quit." Right, left, right, left. There, I just did four more but I'm sure I don't have another one in me. Bad thought! I'd better dissolve it right away or it's over. It *has* to melt because it's destroying my chances. All I have is me, my breath, the pedal strokes, the bicycle and one thousand five hundred more miles. The more miles I cover, the more I understand that the bicycle can never be separated from the human being. It isn't just some object I get on and ride. It's become an extension of my consciousness and my character, of my fingers and my feet and my toes. It's the expression of a mentality so pure and serene, nothing can interfere—except my mind if I allow it to beat me up.

I'm used to getting beaten up. When I was grammar school age, as a symbol of our rising social status my parents enrolled me, a frightened skinny Jewish kid, into a strict and prestigious Catholic boarding school. Once I was there, the pattern of abuse increased. Although I was a motivated athlete I was a terrible student with reading disabilities, good at nothing but finding trouble. I was persecuted mercilessly for being different by a group of poorly disciplined kids, products of their apartheid environment, which lacked morals, humanity and ideals. Domination and pain were all they knew. After all, didn't their ancestors organize and perpetuate some of the worst injustices and oppression on the face of the earth? They regularly beat me up, in groups, and I was too fearful to fight back.

My solace was the fact that my bicycle had no mind of its own. The only thing in my life that didn't oppose me, the bicycle was my saving grace. It never answered back or gave me grief. Even in an injured state this metal structure was my friend, predictable and responsive, and I could read its signals loud and clear. I actually felt its pain when a squeak from the tires told me I was about to get a flat.

In hindsight, sitting on that bicycle saved me. You see, on the road, when the pain comes

It's bad,

and then it's good,

and finally, it doesn't matter.

In the end it is what it is, and I taught myself to use all my techniques and tools to breathe with the pain and let it pass. In the early days, when I sped along the road free from heartbreak, alive in the wind, I felt like I was riding on the coattails of God.

So where is He now? Where is He hiding during this search for sanity in a world that makes absolutely no sense to me? Right pedal stroke, left pedal stroke. I think my eyelids are closing. What if I fall asleep on the bike? I bet my feet'll keep pedaling and as long as I cross that finish line I win, whether I'm awake or asleep. But that doesn't seem right. It wasn't supposed to be like this, this wasn't how my dream looked. I knew the ride would be tough but wasn't it also supposed to be about glory, power, connection and winning? Not isolation and torn-up flesh. What about that time in South Africa when I rode across the country for the black school kids? Why doesn't it feel like that? I dreamed my first dream of glory then, and made it come true and it felt like a piece of heaven.

I was in college, pretty much on the road to nowhere, dabbling with marijuana, dating Busty Bebe the stripper, getting beaten up by the other guys, raiding my father's pharmacy and breaking into his liquor cabinet whenever I had a chance. I had no goals. My mother was the keeper of my dreams until I could hold onto my own. Even without personal dreams though, I couldn't ignore the inhumanity of apartheid. A single black mother was given only about sixteen dollars a month from which she had to feed and clothe her kids as well as buy schoolbooks, pens and all the rest of the supplies that white kids were given for free. When I heard about an organization named TEACH, I suddenly realized that under their auspices I could help someone besides myself. I arranged to ride my bicycle across the country, accepting a set amount of funding per mile that TEACH would distribute to these unfortunate black families. For the first time in my young life I had a purpose beyond my own gratification, and I focused all my attention on it.

I'll never forget the police cars, motorcycle cops and the mayor of Johannesburg leading me out to start that ride. The reporters from the evening newspaper were there, too. It was my first taste of glory when I took off amidst the cheering. As far as I was concerned it could have been the Tour de France, it was such an exciting moment. By the time I reached my destination I'd raised enough money to provide educational materials for one hundred twenty black kids. One hundred twenty. That was two entire classrooms and it was the greatest moment of my life.

Before the ride, I remember staring in awe at a fifties newspaper photograph of several athletes who had crossed the Alps on bicycles in their woolen shirts without leg warmers. Just a few guys facing the elements and themselves. I'd wondered what it would be like to do something so courageous and challenging that your picture would end up on the front page of the newspaper. Suddenly there *I* was on the front page and I felt as close to those climbing champions as I'd ever been. When I first saw it, for a moment I thought I was in *their* photograph standing beside them. I swore then and there that one day I'd be a champion too.

Hey, that looks like Jack again. He's showing up every mile, standing on the road and cheering me on, then getting in his car, riding ahead and doing it again. I'll be seeing him doing this for a long time, probably even when he stops. His image will be a mirage on the road in front of me, joining the rest of the hallucinations that are coming pretty fast and furious now. What do I expect after this many days with so little sleep, almost no money in the bank, minimal sponsorship and even less emotional support? What made me think I could pull this off, that I could withstand the emotional torment, never mind the physical torture?

And who are these guys, the ones balancing on each of my shoulders? I can't see their faces and I don't remember inviting them here, but they won't go away. I don't like what they're saying to me, that I failed in my marriage and that my life isn't worth anything. What do they know about me? These critical thoughts are interrupted by one of my crew, an ex-colonel from Vietnam. I can hear his voice, I can see his lips moving, but I don't understand a word he's saying. All I hear is what he said to me a while back: "Crewing this race is about the sport of watching deterioration and pain." He'd said it with a strange, hungry look on his face and I felt creepy.

Well, he must be getting an eyeful right about now, between the nervous ulcers that broke out all over my skin before the race and my saddle sores, my ruptured Achilles tendon (I think it happened yesterday, whatever that means) and the weight loss. Twenty-seven pounds. I know this is bad. When you ride in the Iron Man competition, if you lose a few pounds they pull you into the medical tent to get you hydrated. But there's nobody to pull me in any direction here in Kansas. Not in *or* out. And I feel heavy as lead while I'm losing body structure, my nose is bleeding and one of my teeth is dissolving. Right in my own mouth. How much more of myself am I willing to give up to cross that finish line? A bit of kidney, a slice of liver, another tooth? My heart? Doesn't matter, it's already broken.

So what gives me the right to expect anyone to be here for me? It's not like this pain is an accident. It's self-inflicted. Why should my loved ones support me while they watch me eat myself alive? There's no prize money at the end, no endorsements. It doesn't even feel like a race. Where are the other contestants? I can't see anyone except that van with those people inside and they're not racing. I'm the only one doing it.

Breathe in, breathe out.

21

A car's passing me. I'm riding in all this open space and I can see people sitting inside that vehicle thinking they're protected. They're not. They're just ants, scurrying from one little shelter to another. And here I am, living in this big outdoors with no roof over my head, riding through rain and snow while little people sit in moving boxes that start and stop with doors that open and close. They get out and quickly move into another box that's disguised as a restaurant or a cinema or a house. They eat their food, watch their movies and lie in their beds, thinking they're safe. I did it my whole life too, moving from one little box to another. But I can see that it's all one big birdcage and I keep breaking through into the next one. And really, even if I could fly I couldn't make it to freedom because there's always another cage. And there's this pedal stroke again, the right and then the left.

I'd better drink more water because I'm losing my body mass. I just scrunched up my eyes to see a gift from heaven up ahead—a mountain. Or a hill. What's the difference? At least it's a change in terrain. I must have left Kansas but I can't imagine when. I remember stopping somewhere a few miles back and Jack bought some raw steaks for me to sit on. Flesh pillows for my decimated butt. It was his idea. I'm a strict vegetarian and since the skin I'm sitting on is torn apart, the essence of that steak is probably creeping right up inside my body and taking over. But the pain is so deep, these horrific slabs of cow I'm sitting on might mean the difference between finishing or not.

The hills are coming up. My legs are burning again. The pain is unbearable but at least I can feel my legs. More than I can say for my toes. They're numb, they've been numb for a few days now and it scares me. Better not tell anyone. There's nothing I can do short of stopping but accept them. Just as they are. Accept and respect my numbed-out toes. Let them go. Watch them do the same old thing even when they're numb, floating the pedal stroke.

I can't afford to lose my tenacity or my rhythm. That's what gives me the enthusiasm to change gears, to go into attack mode so I can soar up over the hill. But I don't want to change gears right now. I'm used to this gear, I feel safe with it—but I can't just sit here pedaling the same old way and expect to get to New York. I have to start attacking again. I'm lonely. It's cold out here all alone. Float the circle of the pedal stroke. My hands are relaxed but my wrists are burning again. My fingers are numb. What's the difference between my numb fingers and my numb toes? I'm getting worried that maybe my hands'll fall off the handle bars. That would be disaster. Better stop thinking about it.

My head's nodding. What if I fall asleep? I can't let my head nod anymore. I want to sleep so badly but sleep's not scheduled for six more hours. No sleep. How good would it feel to have a new pair of shorts and somebody to rub out my legs? I see somebody on the side of the road on a massage table getting his legs rubbed. Is he really there or am I hallucinating? Does it matter? Maybe I should stop now. I can't stand this saddle anymore, it's burning so much. I wanna go home. Why did I decide to do this in the first place? It was supposed to be a good game, but it isn't good at all and now I can't quit.

Here comes the hill. Even though I've dropped twenty-seven pounds in less than a week, it feels like I'm too heavy to take on the mountain. This is my plan of attack, keep the same gear and get so light, so ethereal, I can float right up and over. Or can I? My reality is so distorted now, I'm not thinking right. I'm just breathing and pedaling. Forget one day at a time, it's one heartbeat at a time — with no guarantees.

My life is flashing before me and I know this race isn't what it appears to be. It's not about racing at all. It's a journey of truth, isn't it? It's about facing myself, finding my center, and discovering a way to fit into the world. So this is the conflict, the reason I entered the race. Cyclist of the Month, the magazines called me. What does that mean now? It all seems pretty ridiculous.

I think Indianapolis is coming up. Sometimes it seems like I'm pedaling and breathing and all these cities pass by me instead of me passing by *them*. And Christ is sitting on my left shoulder and Satan is on my right. I knew those guys were familiar. Since I can't find a reason to go on, maybe they can.

Satan says I have to pedal until I drop because I can't let down my sponsors. And what about all the people who didn't offer me any support? He says I have to show them what I'm made of, so they'll respect me.

Christ says I need to make a choice for myself. He says true strength isn't necessarily about finishing. It's also about walking away with my consciousness intact. He says no one can ever take this race away from me because I'll be quitting of my own accord.

"Nobody's holding a gun to his head," Christ tells Satan. "We both know he's in no shape to finish this race. He'll be finishing himself, not the race."

"But the ring," says Satan, "his life won't have meaning without it."

"A ring means nothing," says Christ. "This is about preserving his life."

"But less than twenty people have one," Satan retorts. "It'll be instant respect."

"Respecting himself and his body are much more important."

On and on they go as if I'm not even here. I'm trying to ignore them, to shut them up. Right pedal stroke, left. But what's this now? I'm stopping. Oh dear

23

God, You win. I'm getting off the bike. My crew chief is freaked. He knows this isn't a pit stop. I just took one a few miles back. This is serious.

I hear him telling me we're in Indianapolis. "Four hundred miles from the finish line, Johnny," he says.

Does that mean anything? I'm coming down to earth enough to understand his words. It's as if before I got off the bike, the letters were scrambled beyond recognition. Now they're dropping into enough order for me to vaguely recognize them as words with specific meaning.

"I had no idea what this was," he's saying now.

How could anyone understand? This is beyond understanding, I really didn't get it myself. But now resolution is what it's about. The resolution I should have had before I began. Better late than never, right? I start walking on whatever is left of my legs. Now that the pressure is off, the pain is getting worse. I can barely tell the difference between pain and release, cold and hot. It's all the same and my consciousness is one-pointed. The conflict is over. I'm four hundred miles from the finish line and for me this race is done. The voices have stopped. Thank God. I couldn't bear them any more. I know I'd have gone mad if I hadn't found a way to shut them up.

The person who was driving my car behind the van is getting out. I didn't even realize my car was here. That's good, I can leave in my own car, but there's something I have to do first. I'm reaching into the van, taking the two spare bicycles plus the one I was just riding and dumping them by the side of the road, wheels and all. Now I'm dumping nine hundred bottles of Evian water. My sponsor. Three bicycles and tons of gallons of designer water strewn by the side of the road. Remnants of a dream. Of my undoing.

I hear my crew chief talking to me again. "I had no idea, buddy," he's saying. "If you ever want to do this again, I'll make it up to you." He's a multimillionaire and I have an odd memory of him tossing ten thousand dollars in gold coins in the air before the race started. So what was that supposed to mean?

"It's done, Robby," I'm telling him.

"I mean it," he says, his voice running ahead of him. "I never saw a performance like this in my life. If you ever want to come back, I'll make sure you have everything you need. Money, crew, all of it. Full support."

His arms are moving around to punctuate his words but I'm not bothering to answer. I'm getting into my car and starting up the engine. I have to get away —from him, my crew and the road. Now I'm pointing the car toward home and I'm driving. My legs are cramping, they're getting more painful by the second.

I don't care, I have no context for pain any more. I just hope I don't pass out behind the wheel.

I look out the front windshield. I recognize nothing. It's all a blur, one object bleeding into the next. I'm heading home like a workhorse blindly running for the stable. I have a lot less than when I left. Maybe a lot more too, but I can't evaluate it yet. In two days I'll be home if I don't have to make too many pit stops. I'll deal with my life then.

But wait, I *have* no home. I have two kids, Jason and Jacqueline, my marriage is over, I have nowhere to live and no money to feed myself. I'll worry about that when I get back because that's when the real work starts. I'll have to refurbish my organs and make this body work again so I have the wherewithal to decide if it's worth it for me to go on. I could go to India, sit on a mountaintop and fast until I'm dead. Then it won't make any difference whether or not I'm wearing a RAAM ring. But I have to get strong enough to think clearly. You can't end your life until you can make a clear decision. That much I know.

Back on the road, this time with an engine beneath me. Hey, there's Jack waving, but really, he left days ago. I must be in Kansas again where the ghost of Jack lives, always waving, cheering on crazed cyclists. My legs feel like they're still pedaling, like a sailor who just got off the boat and hasn't gotten his land legs yet. But when I look down, they're still, the right foot pressing down the accelerator, the left one motionless, resting beside it with nothing to do. Pain is shooting from so many parts of my body at the same time, it's impossible to pinpoint where it's coming from. The numbness must be going away. I guess that's a good sign but it's like I'm rising from the dead and it doesn't feel so good. My Achilles tendon is throbbing and something's going on with my back. I don't even want to know what it is. And I feel these fingers of electricity running down the sides of my legs from my thighs to my knees.

Boy, I'm thirsty. Why did I dump all nine hundred bottles of Evian water when I left Indianapolis? I know I wanted to travel light but I should have kept a couple for the ride home. That almost makes me smile but I haven't smiled in so many days, my mouth doesn't know how to form into that shape. It doesn't matter whether I'm thirsty or not. I think I'll go straight to Robby's house, drink a gallon of water and lie down for about three months. If I ever recover from this, I have some figuring to do. I think I need to discover a way to balance my life — if I can find a reason to bother.

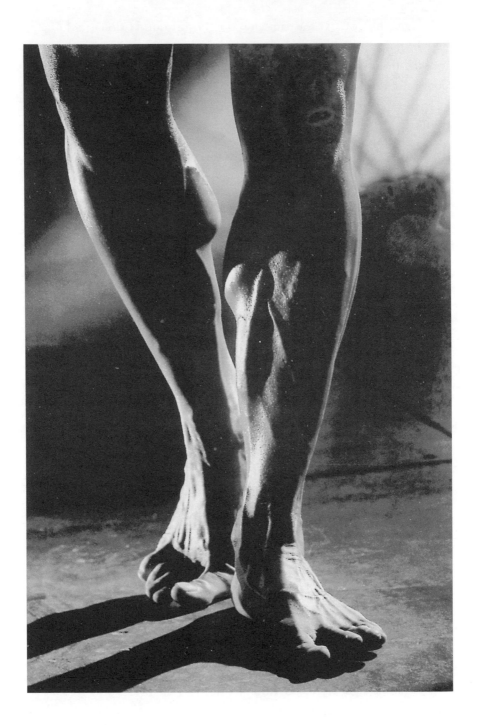

THE FIVE SPOKES OF BALANCE

A Path to Your Inner Truths

IN 1984, an inkling of the Five Spokes of Balance began to flood my troubled mind, although it would be many years and one thwarted attempt at the RAAM before I would be able to synthesize the system. Living by the credo "more is better," my training at that time involved sixty to eighty hours a week on the bicycle—which was far too many. There was no one I could speak with about my problems because I could find no common language. It seemed that neither therapist nor athlete could possibly relate to the fact that I was training for an event that was over two hundred hours long. Needless to say, it was one of the loneliest periods of my life.

During one of my isolated training sessions, when I was riding the one hundred fifteen miles from Santa Barbara to Los Angeles, a spoke on my bicycle broke. I got off the bike and used a special wrench to "true" the spoke, returning it to the proper tension to balance the wheel. When I got back on the bike and passed through the small town of Oxnard, I caught sight of a group of colorful workers in the strawberry fields. I waved to them. When several of them waved back, a new awareness overtook me: There were other people in this world who had their own lives in which everything did not revolve around me. What a revelation for a self-absorbed athlete!

I felt happy as I looked beyond myself into the lives of other people who were engaged in activities that had nothing to do with me. To them, this day wasn't about my life, my training, my bike or my race. They were living their lives, working the fields, and I was living mine, riding the bike. We were all involved in different activities that were meaningful only to us, and we had everything we needed to get through the day. That became my mantra:

Ride the bike and it will give you everything you need.

At that moment, rolling along the road on a well-balanced wheel, I understood that I didn't need to work on my strengths. I had those down. The broken spoke was where I needed to place my attention. In other words, I needed to get specific about my weaknesses. Pertinent questions flooded my mind. Was I aware and conscious in my life? Was I following the right diet? How was my mentality affecting my performance? Were my relationships in order? Was I working efficiently toward my goals and dreams?

As I cycled along the highway, I realized that my deepest motivation wasn't about being the most popular person in the world. A champion athlete rarely comes away from his self-absorbed training with extra friends. It wasn't about making a million bucks either, or becoming famous. Focusing on money or fame would not move the bicycle toward my goals and dreams. Rather, just as the spokes needed to be balanced in order to drive the bicycle forward, I needed to find personal balance without being self-destructive, depressed, anxious or panicked. Then I could relax into the simplicity of today, just as it was, pedal stroke to pedal stroke, while I continued to dream satisfying dreams for the future.

In essence, that was the seed for the Five Spokes of Balance, a path to self-discovery. It was close to three years later, though, as I lay on my back debilitated from my first RAAM attempt, when the structure of the system really started to take form. I was in terrible shape, physically and emotionally destroyed, my entire life in shambles with no idea where I was going. As an athlete, my body was trashed from organ tissue to teeth, all the way into the very cells. As a human being, the structure of my life had caved in as my marriage had fallen apart and I had no home and no money. Without a clue as to what to do next, I accepted an extraordinarily kind offer from my RAAM crew chief, Robert Levin, to recuperate in his guesthouse near Calabassas in the mountains above Malibu.

During this difficult time, unable to walk or clearly communicate my thoughts to anyone, I pondered the connection between physical, emotional and spiritual well-being. I needed to create structure in my life, that much I knew. But how? For a three-month period, I slept and nursed myself back to health while I contemplated my insignificant existence. It was all much too overwhelming. I hadn't ridden a bicycle since the RAAM, I had no aspirations for my future and suicide lay heavy on my mind.

As soon as I could move around again, I called my sister Susan to tell her that I was going to India. But I didn't admit to my plan about fasting on a mountaintop until I disappeared. How could I ever tell her such a thing? As fate would have it, even though I only told her part of the story, this was the most important phone call of my life.

"I'm going to India," I said. "I need some time to be alone and think."

"Go if you want," Susan replied, "but I just met this great person named Jodi. She's crazy, you'd like her. Before you leave, why don't you call her?"

When I heard Jodi's voice on the phone, I knew my life was about to change. We fell in love the moment we met, I cancelled my suicide plans, we married and Jodi helped me find my heart and the love I'd been missing. As I watched this wonderful woman reach outside herself to meet life on life's terms, feed the homeless and offer hope to lost people, I came face to face with the very things that were creating my own imbalances. What had I done for other people lately? I couldn't think of a good answer. Through the force of Jodi's love, I was able to care again, to open my heart to myself and others. I also was able to complete the RAAM in 1989, preceded by the RAAM Open West, a 554-mile qualifier race in which I set the ultradistance record, finishing in twenty-nine hours and forty-six minutes—a record that still stands.

Up until I discovered the Five Spokes, many of the more contemporary philosophies seemed to focus solely on self-preservation as the path to inner peace, to heal wounds and ultimately to connect with God or a higher power. The problem was I felt so bad about myself so much of the time, I didn't believe I deserved that kind of peace and comfort. I searched for a life philosophy that would include the negativity, help me cut through my judgments and give me a semblance of peace and emotional stability. All to no avail. When I realized it didn't exist, I finally made it up. I credit the Five Spokes of Balance as one of my most powerful training tools to guide me through the bad times. The system helped me feel good about myself as a human being and remotivate myself to right action and direction.

The truth is that as much as we wish it were different, most of us must deal with the negative aspects of life before we get to the positive ones. I suppose that's simply a part of being human. But all too often we are encouraged not to acknowledge the negative thoughts. "Let it go, let it flow," we are told. "Move on to something nice, drop the pain, forget about it and it will disappear."

29

My experience has shown me something different. I have found that when I become aware and sensitive to all my emotional shifts, including the negative ones, telling the truth about my feelings allows me the most freedom. Since negativity comes from the inside out, peace arrives by acknowledging its presence and accepting all states of mind as parts of myself. Pretending they do not exist will not make them go away. With this in mind, putting the Five Spokes into practice helped me develop strategies, visualization techniques, and their metaphysical offshoots into which I could sink my teeth during the hard times.

Since all parts of life are interconnected, one tangent affecting the next, the task is to put all of your individual, disconnected parts into balance in order to become a connected, whole, healthy human being. This is the true meaning of fitness, the basis for a normal athlete to become a superathlete. Even more importantly, it's the basis for a fragmented person to become a whole, integrated human being. The Five Spokes was designed with this in mind.

Simply stated, the Five Spokes of Balance is a sophisticated game plan that helped me find my inner truths. Although metaphorical and imaginary, not physical, the concept of the spokes supports the harmonious development of a fundamental structure through which you can lift yourself out of depression, even in the midst of chaos. The system was devised to be complete unto itself, highly adaptable to each individual, available to help you enjoy your life, even when your goals and dreams seem out of reach.

We all need the same stuff in life, so although I write this from my personal perspective with full understanding of my limitations, I would like to offer you this set of coping skills that helped me through some of the hard times. I based the Five Spokes of Balance upon a macrobiotic teaching:

If you want to get the full nutritional benefits of an orange, you can't eat just one slice. The orange grew as a whole so you have to eat the entire fruit in order to receive the wholeness.

Consider the structure of a bicycle wheel. It has a circular shape, the hub is at the center and the spokes are tangential, joined together at the hub and at the outer rim. If one or more of the thirty-six spokes on the wheel become disconnected, the bike won't go. If it does go, it'll shimmy and shake like a bucking bronco until the wheel jams itself into the frame, distorting and bending the brakes. This renders your bike useless, bringing it to a halt or even causing it to toss you off.

kes to drive it?

no human being to express it?

he same: A wheel won't turn with-
e to spoke, just as a human being is
ection.
an intact wheel that belongs to you
hots. Since the spokes are your sole
is dependent upon your under-
nt actions. Just as no spoke in the
is interconnected with the others
. Whether you're embarking on a
ng the beach or a 3100-mile Race
at you can steer in the exact direc-

st inroad to finding my heart was
d from a lack of consciousness and
balance was polluting all the other
iage and my connection with my
ction. All of my relationships were
o overpoweringly out of whack, I
spective.

So which path would I adopt to restore my body, my spirit and my mind, so I could feel better and develop into the superathlete that I'd always dreamed of becoming? I could go the pharmaceutical route, the Zen route, the physiotherapy route. And then there was kinesiology, the old "coach" mentality, and the military zombie route that was all about no pain, no gain. I knew that one. It had put me where I was at that very moment, flat on my aching back, and it had taken a slice of my liver in the process. There had to be a better way.

Since martial arts had already led me in an Eastern philosophical direction, I decided to reach far and deep within myself to embrace the Zen route and develop what is called a "Zen mind." Instead of flipping from one pole to the other, low to high, depression to elation, bobbing around like an apple in a barrel of water, I started to reconstruct my life according to a plan.

The more I brought the Five Spokes of Balance into play and discovered what was true for me, the more my justifications for sickness, manic behavior, relationship problems and lack of sleep became exposed. I was slowly discovering a way to make sense of it all as I took the fragmented parts of myself and fit them into little boxes and columns. Now I had a semblance of a blueprint, some rough and yet dynamic coping skills. I began to discover right perspective, as the areas of decay and weakness in my life become apparent. I saw that strengthening one aspect of my life was no guarantee that I could achieve the balance I needed to cross the finish line. In fact, sometimes when I strengthened one spoke I was draining energy from another. In this way I was actually weakening the whole, an awareness that led me to the fundamental inner truth behind the entire system:

Each and every spoke on the wheel is interconnected and interdependent upon every other spoke.

I now know that when the athlete falls through the cracks and makes fatal errors, it's due to a lack of consciousness, not necessarily a lack of physical preparedness. In fact the physical aspect, although crucial to the whole, often gets dwarfed by the deeper stuff—the emotional pressure, the difficult feelings, self-hatred, insecurities and lack of personal control. Through my exploration, I began to understand that no matter how well prepared I was or how fast I could pedal my legs, I was only as good as how centered I was. I also knew that I had a chance to become a satisfied human being or a superathlete. Whatever my goal, the fundamental task at hand was to make an arrangement between the mind and body. Then and only then could I bridge the gap between being a mere athletic participant and a super champion.

As I strove to balance myself from within, I was intrigued by the popular pyramid concept of mind, body and spirit. I recognized this triad as integral parts of the whole, but I also knew it wasn't the whole picture. Fundamental pieces were missing, such as the subtlety of the emotions and feelings. What about mental misconceptions and distortions? What about incorrect training methods or sudden changes in nutritional needs, daily structure, desires, mood swings and chemical imbalances? And then there were outside distractions and disturbances.

I investigated my life as objectively and vigorously as possible. While I always had pretended to be in control and together, I had to admit that I was actually quite sad; I felt "less than" and I was needy. I had tried covering it up by coming off as superhuman, numbing out, riding hundreds of miles every week, climbing mountains and overtraining. When life was sunny and it was working, it was great. But no matter what I did or how intensely I trained, it got harder and harder to bring up the sunshine. Since the spokes radiate from the core of a person's being, my potential was limited because my core was as yet dark and unexplored.

The more I thought about the mind/body connection, the more desperate I was to find a way to go to sleep at night without being fearful. I wanted to wake up alert and enthusiastic, I wanted to feel good after I ate and I wanted to face myself and know the truth about my feelings. I also wanted to be able to discern the difference between anger, fear, anxiety and insecurity. I needed a way not only to rebuild my physical health, I also needed a life philosophy or a game plan to provide me with a structure for the changing experiences that arose on any given day.

In order to achieve that goal, the structuring of the Five Spokes of Balance became a great source of creativity for my solitude and a saving grace in my daily comings and goings. Being bipolar, my moods switched constantly, so I used the system as a daily point of contact from which to look at myself and make sense of my life. I used it to face my insecurities and to find a way to transform them so I could move toward balance. I was determined to squeeze the last droplets of energy from each spoke in order to balance my life and replace insecurity with inner strength.

As an athlete, insecurity affects everything we do: the way we climb a hill on a bicycle, the gears we choose and how assertive we are. Professional cyclists know that most of the time you don't win a race from the front of the pack. It has to be strategic and energetic at the same time; you hang back, never too far, staying in contact with the whole, conserving energy and waiting for the critical moment. If you're riding in the middle of the pack and you're not assertive when the situation calls for it, you can get pushed from side to side and place yourself and everybody else in jeopardy. I'm not referring to boisterous assertiveness where you shove your way to the front of the pack, running people down in the process. I'm talking about psychological assertiveness, where your ability to cope with stress and make decisions under pressure and pain become critical.

Things happen fast in a pack; there's no time to look back, so you'd better have studied, assessed and distilled the strengths and weaknesses of each of your competitors. Once you're so close you can feel each other breathe, you have to be familiar with individual temperaments and rhythms. You must find a way to liberate yourself in a congested frenzy of one hundred cyclists screaming round

33

a bend in a few seconds, all of you traveling over forty miles per hour, moving on your tires with metal and bodies on every side. This is no picnic at the park —it takes focus, precision, control, calmness, coordination, courage, lots of training and, most of all, a clear mind.

As odd as it sounds, you must have a powerful commitment to an illusion. I'm referring to your ultimate goal to win, which is nothing more than a dream because it doesn't yet exist. Cycling, therefore, is a highly psychological experience. You need to know when somebody in the pack is about to make a move before he or she actually does it. You have to ride with confidence in the middle or at the back of the pack, or at least in a position where you can keep everyone else under surveillance. Then you can use that confidence to dominate, move out or come off the front when the time is right. An indecisive strategy can render your chance of attack hopeless. A lack of inner strength, acting squirrelly and a preponderance of insecurity can cause a serious crash and bring down the entire pack.

In daily life, the same laws apply. If you're insecure or dangerous to yourself, if you don't take advantage of unexpected opportunities in an ethical way, you're likely to compound, confuse and unravel the moment. That will affect everything you do—from a race, to your work, to your relationships, to the way you dream, to the clarity of your consciousness. Imagine being too unaware to make a life-saving phone call to the doctor, too afraid to speak up when someone is treating you badly, or too confused to guide your children when they need you.

This is where the Five Spokes of Balance can help you find a way to extract opportunity from adversity and to transform chaos into liberation in any precise moment. In this modern world, there's enough violence and abuse perpetrated each day to remind us that as a culture we don't have perfect faith or dedication. With society breaking down under a lethal political structure that looks like a fixed game at the wrestling ring, we don't always make choices that are wise, helpful or selfless. We are often motivated by fear, blinded by greed, and we go out of balance in the snap of a finger or in the wake of a single confused thought.

A mere moment of awareness can affect your attitude and change the entire course of the rest of your life. This is where the Five Spokes has offered me a useful and practical system, both in my athletic training and in my daily life. When I first came up with the concept on that awesome ride along the California coast, I considered it my Ninja secret weapon, a tailor-made tool that I've continued to develop for practical use. With help from wonderful teachers and a great therapist, Dr. Don Freeman, I utilize the spokes to this day to evaluate my own state of well-being. I don't always find solutions, but the system offers me a ray of hope that can light up an otherwise dark situation or enhance an already good situation and make it great. It also offers me a semblance of sanity amid the chaos that often threatens to shake up the very foundations of my life. Perhaps it can help you, too.

I've identified the five spokes as follows:

Spoke #1. Consciousness
Spoke #2. Nutrition and the Body
Spoke #3. Mind: Thoughts, Emotions and Feelings
Spoke #4. Relationships
Spoke #5. Goals and Dreams

Since I initially found my freedom on a bicycle, the bridge between my life and the Five Spokes of Balance was inevitable. Maybe there are other roads I could have traveled to get to the same end. There are many ways to go, but since this was the one I chose, allow me to offer it to you now. In the development of your awareness, as you choose your own way and find your own inner truths, please enjoy my insights. Integrate them into your own life if that feels appropriate. You never know, there may be something here that will be workable for you.

In exploring the individual spokes, keep in mind that movement in any one spoke will affect all the others in the most subtle of ways. As we bring the spokes into balance one by one, your insights into yourself may surface, which are different for everyone. Each individual's inner truths are personal, and yet in the end we are all striving to arrive at the same destination—a balance of body, mind and spirit as well as that of thoughts, emotions and feelings. May we all be blessed today and every day with such a miracle.

As we go on to discuss each spoke at length, please remember:

You cannot get fit in one training session. You cannot live your life in one day. Trophies come and go. Your body ages and your performance eventually will decline. No matter if you are in denial, or how much you train, you can do nothing to reverse these universal laws. What you can do is investigate your spokes, discover their meaning and dream beautiful dreams for yourself, your loved ones and everyone you touch.

My garden

CONSCIOUSNESS

I VIEW CONSCIOUSNESS as the universal idea that something unreachable is out there, creating the tiny seed that makes a blade of grass grow. I believe it is a good idea to work on expanding our consciousness but no matter how hard we try, we can't create the seed. Herein lies a fundamental awareness about consciousness that has excited me and led me down a metaphysical path of exploration. I've always been fascinated by the elusive force that makes the orange tree bear fruit each year at almost the same time—the idea that without a seed there is no tree and the seed is inside the orange. When we accept the fact that we can plant the seed but we can't replace the seed or understand how it landed on otherwise barren land, we are recognizing and yielding to an essence in this world that is far greater than ourselves.

As we drop resistance to this fundamental truth, we are provoking our consciousness in the form of deep thoughts, ideas and insights: the teachings of the first spoke. Balancing the consciousness spoke allows a person to go deeper than muscle strength or a confused mind. It inspires greatness and supports an ability to overcome personal limitations. When you believe that your life path is only about the ride, the condition of your body, your life structure, your values, your business or your health, what will you fall back on when the pain gets too great? What will happen to you when a tire blows out? Or worse, when your mind or your life turn against you? How will you find the tenacity to see the truth when you're chin-deep in adversity?

The answer to each of these questions arrives when we find the strength and courage to choose right action and get to the other side. While conscious awareness is a powerful resource for finding enough faith and hope to overcome physical and mental obstacles, the lack of conscious awareness is often a great cause of suffering. For example, after I arrived in America and began training celebrities, my life should have been great. It certainly looked that way. I had a good gig working in the elite Malibu colony. Although my family had been relatively well off in South Africa, I was being exposed to riches the likes of which I'd never imagined. I was spending time in magnificent mansions, privy to the inside conversations and coercions of the biggest Hollywood players. Cool, I'd really made it and I had plenty to write home about. Right?

I'm afraid that was only half the story. The problem was that I had a secret. While I was making good money motivating people to find happiness within themselves and giving them a reason to get up in the morning, I was wishing I was dead. I'd burned out because I had no connection to or awareness of my consciousness. I was not paying attention to my needs. I was working too much, I took no personal time and I was obsessed with getting somewhere. The trouble was, I didn't know where.

When I was thirteen years old, preparing for my bar mitzvah in South Africa, the issue of consciousness was already up for review. I'd learned all the words in Hebrew that I was meant to recite, I could rattle them off without a mistake, but I was never taught the meaning, so rattling is exactly what I was doing. The Buddha texts posit the notion that to learn words without their meaning is like seeing a lily without smelling its fragrance. In speaking meaningless words, I never had the opportunity to embrace the flower for its essence. It seemed crazy to dedicate so much time and effort to the practice and study of a bunch of sounds. I am aware that was my father's way and the way of those who came before him, but I never tuned into the consciousness behind the effort.

As I continued to repeat what the rabbi told me were "holy words," admonishing me to treat them as such, it became problematic in my thinking. I wanted to talk to God in my own language with my own feelings. I wanted to be sincere and to have the privilege of knowing what I was saying. If these meaningless words didn't move my heart and soul, how could I perceive them as holy? What did "holy" mean, anyway? At that point, religion and spirituality became something extraordinary to me and my search for meaning began in earnest. Without knowing it, I'd begun working to balance the first spoke.

In my experience, balancing the five spokes is not a finite task because balance is never set in stone. From my perspective, it's a dynamic process that moves back and forth constantly, something that is worthwhile looking at and checking into as we travel along this road of life. A sense of balance comes to us at times when we least expect it and then it leaves. But the memory of being centered can add to our arsenal of tools when we find ourselves out of whack.

I had an experience of conscious awareness in high school, the memory of which still nourishes me. It was my first taste of freedom when I rode my bicycle four hundred miles, halfway across South Africa, to raise money for poverty-stricken black children who wanted to go to school but had no means. It was there on the road that I found a sense of myself. I also found rhythm in the left pedal stroke and then the right as I traveled from feeling to feeling and finally from breath to breath. This rhythm came and went, it showed up suddenly and promptly disappeared, but it was there and it was mine, no longer hidden so far away as to be inaccessible. I'd tasted the balance of my consciousness, which spurred me on to greater hope in a life that previously had been bereft of satisfaction or appreciation. At the end of that ride I was permanently changed. I would spend the rest of my life remembering and working to recreate the same sense of conscious awareness.

When the awareness of consciousness is hidden or out of balance, it creates havoc. The mind takes over and becomes the ruler, and it is a pretty fickle and dangerous king. Have you ever noticed that your mind is happy when it's happy and then suddenly it switches and becomes grouchy with no apparent explanation? For example, you're having a good day until the phone rings. Someone starts yelling at you for no reason you can understand and suddenly you're angry. You fill up with resentment, you lose your focus and you spend the rest of the day upset. The mind shifted in a moment and it may not shift back for hours. Clearly, the mind is an inaccurate barometer for consciousness. It can only project experiences based on the past, which in turn creates feelings that have no basis in reality. The mind simply knows what it knows, it attracts what it attracts, and everything it doesn't know or attract lives in the peripheral.

The bicycle presents an excellent metaphor here. If you get aggressive with it, it behaves aggressively. If you're not paying attention and you hit a pothole, it'll jolt you awake. If you're aware enough to avoid the pothole, you get a smooth ride no matter what went before. It's not about being fickle. Rather it's a case of pure cause and effect, something you can count on. This demonstrates the difference between having faith in the power of the mind and having faith in universal consciousness, two wildly and yet subtly opposite ideas.

Prior to my working with the rich and famous in Hollywood, I had never trained to look good or feel good. Rather I'd used my training and my mind solely to punish myself mercilessly and to evoke performance. In a desperate search for acknowledgment and love, I had trained in order to feel pain, which was what I thought I deserved. The bigger and stronger I became, the harder I beat up on myself. As a result, I never felt fit enough, fast enough or strong enough, let alone happy enough.

It's clear to me now that my consciousness was critically out of whack, and yet all roads lead to the same place. Through the eventual awareness that my consciousness was nowhere, I began the process of healing myself enough to find it. I learned that it was through consciousness, not mind, that I could develop the quality of awareness that would lead me to form and structure in my life.

In the end, your life will reflect back exactly the way you treat yourself and others. When you're on the road, for instance, the mile you're riding is all there is. Or at least it should be. This is where the mind tries to project your experience of the past onto the present, which can dangerously mess with your consciousness. If your mind is bouncing like a pinball in your head, how will you keep your thoughts clear, since your mind knows only the past? What if the mile your mind projects is the toughest one you ever rode? That's not going to help you win a race.

As you attempt to carve your way through the jungle of life, remember that the mind will offer an immature, narrow path, laden with dense confusion. If you use consciousness as a machete, you can cut through it all, making your way slowly, directly and meticulously to the light at the end of the harrowing journey. If you have an inkling of a good direction, once you make that machete your own, with right intention and belief in yourself you can achieve the impossible.

Consider entering into a relationship without consciousness. Your undisciplined mind will project your last lover onto your present one, which will not help you maintain a bond. To move forward, you take the lessons learned and let go of the stories that came before. If you use your awareness to see the truth about where you are in this present moment, you can take right action accordingly. If you can feel the human being sitting across from you, you can respond from your heart, not your mind. Then you can create a structure, a frame of reference or a life philosophy that makes sense.

Remember:

A life without a philosophy is a life without consciousness. A life without consciousness is no life at all.

Appreciation of conscious awareness comes hard sometimes. In 1998 I suddenly fell ill, so ill that for a moment it seemed that I'd lost all consciousness. Of course it was there (where could it go?) but without awareness, I couldn't access it. For seven endless days, my life no longer mirrored my previous mentality or what I knew about the world. During this pivotal time, my attention reverted to physical matter, mere flesh and bone. My consciousness as I knew it had disappeared. My only focus was the desire to survive, to hang on to see another day. In layman's terms, the taffy had stretched so far it had snapped and my life was no longer about esoteric values. Forget about finding nirvana or contemplating life after death. I was reduced to base survival, hanging on to take a breath, another and then hopefully another.

After about a week in this delicate state, awareness of my consciousness began to return. During the subsequent healing process I came to truly understand and appreciate the importance of the first spoke. I'd come away with more than just my life. I had gained an understanding of the most basic human struggle to stay alive and aware. I could appreciate consciousness in a brand new way, truly knowing that without consciousness and understanding I had nothing.

Hopefully you won't have to follow my lead by going to the bottom of the pit in order to expand the perspective in which you see your life. There are other ways to accomplish this same goal. Before you go down like I did, why not start where you are to declare your conscious purpose as love, essence and commitment to the game? When you can see yourself and your actions in a more conscious and honest way, you are free—to make your own decisions based upon your personal understanding and instinctual trust.

To sum it up, the only way to change behavior is to change consciousness. Once you start seeing yourself and your life in an aware fashion, your perspective expands and you can begin to act differently. When the first spoke is in balance for the athlete, the purpose for training is no longer that of punishment, vengeance or proving something. There's nothing to carve out to define your life, there's nothing to show and nobody to show it to. Winning and losing take a back seat to waking up enough to enjoy every moment of the game all along the way. It's like bench pressing with the mind. The more you work on it, the clearer and more expansive it will become. With your consciousness in balance, the need for external power, glory or self-aggrandizement go out the window. You become focused on what you know about drive, purity, commitment and awareness. Once you taste that kind of freedom, you can never go back.

A pear is a pear

the second spoke
NUTRITION AND THE BODY

Beauty is not measured solely by the way you look physically or the way you act. I think it's a combination of the two, when you're so aware you can move gracefully through your life with consciousness, etiquette, character and good health. This requires the merging of the first and second spoke.

As we strive to marry each spoke with the next, we are beginning to form a structural network that will carry us through our lives. For the athlete, it takes consciousness and awareness to create balance with your training time, family time and alone time. And, of course, it takes eating the foods that will allow you not only to perform well but also to feel and look good in the process. The athlete who chooses to nourish him– or herself consciously will feel good about nutritional choices, will not have the urge to starve and then binge, and will come away from training regenerated, not depleted.

Just as you feel the depletion of your spirit when you lack awareness (nobody cares, nobody notices), you also suffer depletion of the physical body when you lack the proper nutrition and hydration. In keeping with an innate desire to be conscious, you can decide how to fuel your body according to how you want to feel. Rather than bombarding yourself with the least expensive and most available type of processed fuel, you can stop and make conscious choices. Why not ingest the very best fuel that will assist you in taking the body where you want it to go, while strengthening your immune system, oxygenating the blood, developing the heart and lungs and working on good circulation? Joints that are both strong and flexible will help you age with grace as you improve yearly like a fine wine. As you mature, why not become soft and more elastic rather than brittle and hard? The choice is yours.

In the early part of my athletic career, I was heavily involved in bodybuilding. When I switched to cycling, my nutritional spoke became confused. Just as the consciousness spoke is in a constant state of flux, so is the nutritional spoke. As my food requirements shifted from taking the body mass up to trimming it down, the question was how to achieve this in a healthy, balanced way.

As I looked for answers, there were so many opinions it was staggering.

From an athletic point of view, whether you're building up or trimming down, the idea is to create as little waste as possible. You want your system functioning cleanly so that you can reap the full benefits from what you eat, easily utilizing what you need and getting rid of what you don't. This takes a combination of consciousness and good nutrition, the marriage of the first and second spoke, as you make informed choices about food.

As with most decisions, it all starts with common sense. If there's sodium nitrate in the meat to preserve it, a conscious person wonders what it will do to the muscle structure. Carcinogenic matter ultimately will not serve the body or the mind. Organic food is an obvious choice, and common sense can be a loyal and dependable guide. I expect that during the next few years, as we achieve greater awareness and consciousness, we will react more to chemicals in our food because we will feel more in general.

Since food is not my clinical area of expertise, you may want to look further for scientific information concerning nutrition. If you don't want to go into this topic in depth, what I can say simply is that if you eat badly and your cholesterol is high, you won't be feeling or performing well. In other words, if you feel good and your body just performed up to your expectations, chances are you've been eating right. On the other hand, if you feel dehydrated, heavy, sluggish or bloated, chances are you're not eating right. If you wake up in the morning and your eyes are glued together because there was too much MSG in your dinner the night before, you might want to eat some natural, healthy food today —like an apple. When you look at the ingredient label, an apple is an apple. It really is that simple. If you're cautious and check the labels, you won't be making too many mistakes. The bottom line is that spinach is spinach, a tomato is a tomato and nitrates are nitrates. That's the long and the short of it.

In the past, I made my food choices for all the wrong reasons. I looked at food and herbs not as a way to heal my body and my emotions, but rather as a way to stimulate my body for performance. I didn't think about how I would feel at the end of the day. I was only interested in winning, so I treated my body like an abused racehorse. Pump in the foods that will stimulate the best performance —as long as he wins, you can always shoot him at the end of the race.

Today I've learned to eat foods for regeneration, not stimulation. The difference is that regenerating foods help me to build a base for my future, not just to serve as a jump-start for one particular race or event. In this way, a depleted organ can come back stronger rather than breaking down even more. This is the true meaning of longevity — feeding the body nutrition that will reduce pressure and allow you to remain healthy and vital for the years to come.

Although nutrition is often considered a simple spoke, it can get confusing because there are so many ways to go. My shift to cyclist required me to throw out most of what I already knew. Basically it felt like I was starting from scratch. What nutrients did I need to run a marathon? How much protein did I require for that amount of increased energy output? Should I be a vegetarian? What about carbohydrates? Did I need more or less than before? How would I determine the answers to these questions in the face of so many different opinions that were prevalent at the time?

I needed to base my decisions upon information but there were too many theories floating around, some good and some bad. In order to balance the second spoke, I decided to think like a pharmacist. (My dad was a pharmacist and they say we eventually become our parents.) I began experimenting with nutrients and foods that would give me strength and stamina, remove waste from my system and calm my mind. I eventually turned to personal experience and body feedback to figure out what worked. That was the only way I could determine my personal needs in the light of the varied systems and dogmatic opinions that were touted and published in the numerous fitness magazines throughout the athletic community.

I quickly learned to consider food not as filler but as fuel. It's all in the way I decided to treat myself. For example, when I adopted the philosophy of food as fuel, I started looking at myself as a Ferrari Testarosa, not a Volkswagen Bug. Although we're all different and so are our needs, I think we'd all agree that choosing the cleanest form of fuel with the least contaminants, pesticides and radiation will be easiest for the body to process. Good nutrition, therefore, isn't all about burning fat and how much food you eat — it's about activity and utilization of the nutrients in the food. For the athlete, it's also about performance as you take a fuel and learn to extract the most from it.

My typical breakfast these days might be brown rice, which is a natural, well-balanced diuretic that makes the body look and feel good, mixed with — no, not milk — carrot juice. Contrary to the advertising campaign that suggests that "milk does a body good," I've found that dairy products tend to clog up my arteries. Carrot juice on the other hand cleanses my arteries, is excellent for the liver, and its high glycemic index offers my body healthy sugars for energy. I choose a breakfast that gives me good carbohydrates in a neutral grain that isn't too acidic or alkaline. And it stays with me.

If what you put in your mouth is creating emotional trauma, then it's safe to conclude that the second spoke is creating trouble and needs to be tweaked. Getting back to common sense, the best gauge for the second spoke of nutrition is whether or not you put the thumb up after you eat. If you feel sluggish and heavy or a little depressed after a meal, it was probably a bad one. If you're too frenetic after a training session, maybe you didn't eat enough. You can use your own body reactions as biofeedback. Really, that's the most accurate gauge there is.

Because the nutritional spoke is so varied, it's also one of the most interesting as it relates so immediately to body image, self-image and performance image. The exerciser is worried about looking good, obsessed with fat and cosmetic concerns, and probably doesn't enjoy eating. The athlete, however, has a much better time not being concerned with fat or looks. It's all about performance and how much snap you feel in your legs. You naturally look good as a by-product of being active in your life, nourishing yourself thoughtfully and keeping your own best interests in mind.

The nutritional journey for the conscious human being, athlete or otherwise, is one of getting the most out of each moment. It's about reaping the rewards of commitment and dedication to being well nourished. It's about exploring all the possibilities at any given moment and thereby experiencing life at its peak and its clarity.

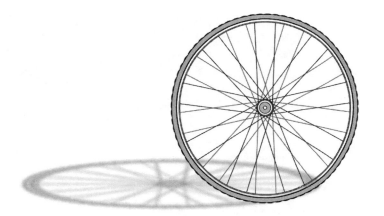

Andrea and me in mindfulness

MIND: THOUGHTS, EMOTIONS AND FEELINGS

I N 1999 I did a weekend seminar and training session in Indianapolis, Indiana. I've done seminars all over the world since I started the Spinning program, but this time something was different. For more than ten years this city had loomed in my consciousness and my mind as the place where I confronted failure for the first time by quitting my first Race Across America.

The truth is, I'd already been quitting on myself for years but I didn't know it. Maybe I didn't want to know it. I was living my life upside down, unaware that I was doing so and unwilling to acknowledge my thoughts, emotions and feelings. My mind simply did not want to allow my feelings and emotions into conscious awareness. It wasn't until I had achieved some degree of balance that I could admit how I truly felt about revisiting this city.

Back in 1987, halfway through my first RAAM attempt, I began to lose my mind. With every pedal stroke, every breath and each ensuing mile, I became more and more confused. My third spoke was so far out of balance, the journey became all about confusion and suffering. My thoughts turned in on themselves and before I knew it I was so filled with negativity, there was no hope of crossing the finish line. Instead of creating open space by cutting the wind in front of me, this bladed spoke was cutting *me* until I was hopelessly severed from the core of my own intention. My mind was polluted, my ducks were not in a row that year and I had no game plan to deal with my problems, my mind or my body. The outcome was preordained: there was no way I could finish.

It seems that a lot of us go pretty far out of our way to ignore our thoughts, emotions and feelings—especially hardheaded athletes. When the third spoke of mind is off balance, the development of the whole athlete as well as that of the human being is in jeopardy. It's all about avoiding feelings, as if that kind of vulnerability would cause us to lose. It couldn't be further from the truth. Repressed thoughts and feelings are the greatest cause of failure, while an open and vulnerable mind is a flexible, winning mind, ready to rearrange itself and do what is necessary in the moment. The trouble is that confronting fear with an open mind and heart takes a brand of courage many people are not willing to muster.

In my case, in order to block my true feelings I created a figurehead, a superathlete called "Johnny G." I did it so effectively, I actually believed in him and used to refer to myself in the third person. I was presenting myself more like a fitness machine than a human being, fancying myself invulnerable and able to suffer tremendous amounts of pain without complaining. When I look back, I wonder why I considered that something of which to be proud. While Johnny G defied nature and pulled off training sessions and all-nighters that would have made the normal athlete go down, where was Jonathan Goldberg, the man with a heart and soul who could be hurt? What had I done with my vulnerable mind, ripe with thoughts, emotions and feelings that could be triggered, and that affected the way I felt about myself and my life? Of course it came and got me in the end. A machine has no emotional breaking point, no off-switch to give off signals that the mind is about to snap. When my mind finally snapped, I nearly went along with it.

I've always maintained that the body follows the mind. If I'm riding on a one-track cliffside with a sheer drop and I think about falling, I'm gone. If I keep my mind on the current pedal stroke and the road ahead, I'll make it back home. You see, the body *does* follow the mind. That's where the emotions and feelings come into play, each of these elements inextricably woven together, separating the man from the machine.

I understand the mind to be, among many things, a tightly netted cluster of emotions and feelings that stimulate thoughts which in turn stimulate physical and nervous responses. When I was a teenager I fell in love with a vibrant, wonderful fifteen-year-old girl named Kay. She was my best friend, always there for me during the abuse and difficulty of my early years. When I was nearly twenty, my mother told me I had to break up with Kay because she wasn't Jewish. Out of touch with my feelings and wanting to please my parents, I told Kay that I couldn't see her any more.

She hid in her room for weeks, unable to sleep, fasting and crying, her emotions so dominating her life that her mental capacities began to decline. So did her body. When she finally emerged, her skin was sallow and her bones stuck out, all luster and vibrancy gone. I, on the other hand, disguised my grief by getting on my bicycle and engaging in a series of abusive rides, creating enough outer pain to mask my inner pain. My approach might have been different, and people might have thought I was okay, but I actually fared no better than Kay. Maybe I fared worse, as the repression of my emotions only added to the burden on my heart that eventually surfaced much later in my life. At least Kay was expressing herself, even if that expression was dramatically off balance.

This story demonstrates two different ways in which emotions and thoughts can weaken the body, whether you're sending them outward or holding them inside. Since performance is dictated by emotions and thoughts, the athlete moves in the direction of cultivating a clear mind. It usually follows that the better the athlete, the clearer the emotions and the more liberated the performance.

Often though, our emotions aren't clear because the mind has been effectively programmed for failure. For instance, I feel pain and a storehouse of repressed thoughts emerge, reminding me of a time when the pain was so great that I couldn't move forward. If I don't reprogram my mind, pretty soon I'm paralyzed and I quit. It's all about negative association.

Heat?

Can't handle it because I remember not being able to handle it once before.

Sleep?

Can't compete because once when I slept badly, I couldn't finish the race.

Irritation?

Somebody said something that pissed me off and now I'm too upset and resentful to pull myself back together.

When the mind is off balance, a simple word can create a ripple effect. The athlete can either be destroyed or encouraged, and the human being can either accept or punish him- or herself. In this way, the third spoke can be a dangerous one, a double-edged sword that cuts through the air like lightning, causing our thoughts, emotions and feelings to work both ways. It all depends on the balance and discipline of the mind. This brings us back to what I call the Taffy Syndrome:

I don't go far enough, the taffy doesn't stretch and I get nowhere.

I go too far, the taffy stretches, snaps, and the mind and body break down.

I surrender, the taffy stretches but before it snaps, it returns
    to its elastic state.

I can read the signs; I know when to speed up, when to back off,
    and I'm free.

When the third spoke is off balance, one of a million different thoughts, emotions or feelings can throw me off track. As Andrea and I work on this book today, we're sitting in my garden among abundant rose bushes. Birds are singing, kids are splashing in the pool and all is well. And yet, a feeling is gnawing at me, contaminating my mind and my body. It's about my mother—the seventh anniversary of her death is around the corner and I never went to her funeral. Unless I acknowledge my regret, no matter how succulent the oranges on the tree growing beside us, my third spoke will be out of balance, my mind will be contaminated with negativity and I won't have peace in my day.

The process is ongoing. You don't just balance yourself one day and that's it. Let's say I returned to Indianapolis, I had a fabulous experience (which I did), and I successfully shifted my evaluation of this city from failure to rebirth. My mind is now healed and clear and all is well, right? Now I should have had no trouble falling asleep. Right?

So why did I toss and turn all night after Indianapolis was over? Since balancing the spokes is a dynamic experience, not a stagnant one, even after befriending Indianapolis, I was nervous about facing a future twelve-hour Spinning journey. Ever since I'd set it up, my emotions and thoughts had been trying to program my body not to get through it. I was thinking defeating thoughts like: I recently recovered from an injury so I'm not functioning at peak performance level. I'm thirty pounds overweight. I haven't been on the road for months.

Indianapolis had no bearing on my present situation. My mind spoke was out of balance once again as it tried to create every possible negative scenario and reason why I should expect failure. A part of me even wanted to cancel the journey, but I knew that one hundred fifty people would be arriving from all over the world, counting on me to lead them through an inspirational ritual for which they'd been training for months.

This is when I turned to the Five Spokes.

The teaching says:

Use your consciousness to nourish your body and change your thoughts in order to balance your mind.

I did this diligently for several months and the results were indisputable: my focus was clear, my weight was normal and my heart rate was back down where it should be. In essence, my emotional structure was back in place and my mind spoke was returning to balance. I knew in my heart and soul that if I could keep my thoughts, emotions and feelings clear, I could get strong and eventually perform well. In the end I not only got through it, it was a rewarding experience for me and for the other participants.

It's all about creating enough space to feel everything, to acknowledge the emotions and to think healthy thoughts. It doesn't matter how it looks on the outside. My eventual success or failure is all about choice and intention. The monk who has three robes and a rice bowl, although he may appear impoverished, actually has a great deal of inner space. He's a wealthy man in his heart, he knows his greater purpose and his consciousness is ripe with options for the future. His mind is in balance, his thoughts are clear and his emotions and feelings are programmed well. His mind is flexible and he is poised for success in whatever he undertakes.

The greedy businessman, on the other hand, overburdened with expectations and a voracious appetite to accumulate more and more things, has no inner space at all. His mind is rigid, his thoughts are tainted, his emotions are repressed. He is poised for failure as he has removed his options and has lost the ability to balance himself. His only hope is to return to the hub of the wheel: self. He must ask himself: What is my greater purpose here? Am I fulfilling it? Is there a reason to carry on and find a different way?

When it all gets too hard, you need to find a reason to keep moving. If the purpose of your journey is not merely to save face, to make your mark, to prove superiority or to aggressively dominate, you'll have a better chance of achieving a balanced mind. With your consciousness clear, your body strong and your emotions freed up, you get to move on to a greater purpose: the satisfaction of ethically completing a commitment to self. This offers you the contentment of feeling fit, healthy, nurtured, nourished, loved and whatever else makes your life worth living. Then you can do anything—a one-legged man can complete the Race Across America, which has actually happened, just because he thinks he can and his spokes are balanced.

Thought, not light, is the fastest medium in the universe. When intention is scattered and fragmented, even if you're all the way there in your body, your negative thoughts will take you out of the race. When the third spoke is in balance, your intention is being directed by a healthy mind.

We all have disturbing emotions and thoughts that challenge us to go deeper, no matter who we are, no matter what we believe. We must remember that just because we can't physically touch our minds, that doesn't mean we should take it for granted. Believe me, the "untouchable" senses are highly capable of throwing the mind into a frenzied chaos—I know this from direct experience. That's why placing your attention on balancing your mind is crucial to the balance of the whole.

With the third spoke in balance, with the mind in harmony with inner space, we have the opportunity to manifest our beauty and strength from the inside out. We are flexible and hopeful. We can appreciate the magic of being human, of having access to awareness, consciousness, passion and a balanced mind. Then and only then do we have the opportunity to experience sheer joy.

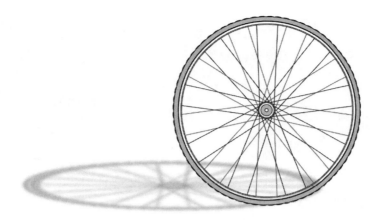

Jodi and me: heaven on earth

RELATIONSHIPS

When I first began to explore the fourth spoke, my only relationship was with my bicycle. Forget about relating to myself or anybody else. I was as numb as the metal I was riding, I showed no appropriate response to other people and I had almost no awareness of my feelings or any other kind of sensitivity. I felt trapped by the fourth spoke, the toughest one for me, because my early life gave me no tools, verbal or otherwise, to deal with other people. For me, this spoke was down from Day One. Needless to say, I had some work to do.

Relating to other people can be daunting when you come from a damaged place, as so many of us do. Feeling threatened, becoming defensive, not being able to recognize the source of what's being fired at us, fear of intimacy, commitment or trust—these are the challenges we face in relationship. The results of abuse in a person's life such as rape, violence, getting your head stuffed down a toilet or whatever else your poison may have been, shows up in this spoke for healing.

In my youth, I didn't trust anybody so I stayed isolated. I felt safer that way, but too much disconnection can distort the nature of reality. Isolation often evokes the sensibilities that come with war, such as desensitization, desocialization and dishonesty, like smiling when you're not happy. Far too often, when the athlete is isolated, you punish yourself and revert to abusing drugs and steroids, losing the link between your true character and what you put forth as your public persona.

Above all else, it's important to remember that when an athletic event is over, you can leave with your trophy but you can't take it to dinner or to bed with you. With a buddy, whether you win or lose the race or the business deal, you can catch a good meal at the end of the day and have a laugh. The difficulty here is that the athlete's relationships often end up sour because of self-obsession. We all know that a one-sided friendship dissolves; it has to be more than a cheering forum in one direction. Herein lies a serious difficulty for the competitive athlete, as you must first and foremost be an athlete—especially if you have your sights set as high as a gold medal or being world champion. The degree of self-absorption it takes to be the best of the best usually creates relationship conflict, which you must find a way to avoid so you won't be distracted from your goals. If you can't have an honest relationship with the people around you, you're better off remaining on your own, keeping your attention on the game. At the same time, as I already said, too much isolation is dangerous. This is where the delicate balance of the fourth spoke can remain elusive.

As a human being who wants to stay centered, athlete or not, you do whatever is necessary to keep yourself in balance. You recognize the value of real friendships and what they add to your life. You may train diligently and yet you still want to be able to find camaraderie and a life that's greater than just training or winning and losing. We all need another person to pull us out of the black holes into which we tend to fall. Winning is not only about being the best. When you look at it philosophically, you can take first, second or eighth place; you can make the deal or it can pass you by; you can fight with your spouse or work it out; but if you're present and honest, you can't really lose. Not if you give it your all. When you wholeheartedly participate in the game, you understand that the fame and mystique of being a champion who always wins is an illusion.

If you're someone who suffers from a dissociated or abusive childhood and being with other people feels completely out of the question, I suggest getting a dog or a cat. I mean it seriously. When you can't relate to anything besides your own pain, helping someone in worse shape than you are can be a gateway to intimacy and relationship. A good way to start relating with something or someone outside of yourself is to find a dog, a cat or a foster child, someone a little smaller and more needy than you. The world is abundant with those who need help, and serving someone less fortunate than you can revitalize your spirit, enlivening the present moment with purpose.

A hidden truth behind the fourth spoke is that without human connection, you can't find what you need to win or even to play the game well. Participation in cycling, running, swimming or business requires strategy, timing and rhythm, all of which are human elements. You really need someone you trust to cheer you on when you're up and to be there when you're down. Without friends keeping each other in check, we will never learn to control the insanity and sickness that can build up and prevent us from finding satisfaction.

Over the years, as I accomplished my athletic goals, achieved a certain degree of fame and allowed people into my life, my relationship spoke still suffered. True, the isolation was over and it was a first step. The problem was that I'd begun to attract a number of people who were insecure and damaged. These so-called friends were living vicariously through me because they weren't out there creating their own lives. As a result they had nothing to give, so although they verbally supported my process they were dependent upon me to keep doing what I was doing so they could survive. That put a great deal of pressure on me. As you can see, the fourth spoke requires intricate investigation and awareness in order to achieve balance.

Try taking your friends out on a bike ride and go over some easy drills with them. Introduce them to your world. Show them your techniques and training methods. On my recovery days, I enjoy taking my mates out and giving them a taste of what I do when I go to work. Once they understand, they respect my training, my schedule, my dedication, and they often feel inspired. That adds a new dimension to our relationship and, believe me, a little understanding can go a long way. When you allow your friends to experience firsthand what your life is about, you may not have to get blindsided into facing your death like I did, in order to change.

The truth is that when someone really loves you, if you honor and trust that love, they never cast you out. You live on forever, even after you die, in a friend's heart and soul — the ultimate longevity.

When I got sick at the height of my career, people began to judge me for my state of mind, attacking Johnny G, never taking Jonathan Goldberg into consideration. They looked at me with shame and embarrassment, actually avoiding me when I walked into my own gym, pretending not to notice me, which was painful and humiliating. I was terribly disappointed when I discovered how many people had befriended me for what I had to offer instead of for who I was. After I cancelled scheduled events all across the country, I looked around and there was my family and a few loyal friends by my side. As difficult and uncomfortable as this time was, my wife and kids gave me everything I had ever dreamed about. My years of dedication to my family paid off.

Let's take a look at five maxims that I value in all of my relationships, both with myself and with others.

The first is CHARACTER.

When I look at the various medals and trophies I've won in races and other competitions, I feel great pride — all except for a bronze medal I received many years ago. When I was competing in the world's shortest, toughest triathlon, I lost my second-place standing by crashing my bicycle and losing large chunks of skin off my body. Terrifically discouraged and in a great deal of pain, I got back on the bike, finished the race and received a bronze medal. It was for fourth place, which should have been a great accomplishment considering the crash. I claimed third place on my résumé, though, and spoke it publicly so many times I started believing it. The truth is that whether it was third or fourth, it made absolutely no difference to anybody else. They really didn't care, but I did. When I walked away with fourth place and called it third, I went from being disappointed to feeling ripped off, to lying, and finally to being ashamed of myself. This was a character problem, one of the symptoms of an unbalanced fourth spoke.

When you can't accept your accomplishments as they are, you can't accept yourself. There's no honesty, no integrity, no trust, no value and of course no peace. The ability to be honest comes through developing character, which the athlete must work on every single day. Included here are the issues of pharmacology, drugs and steroids, as well as groping mechanisms like hanging on to vehicles in a race or any other devious means to get first place. If you end up winning without really deserving it, you'll always know in your heart that the trophy doesn't belong to you.

The second maxim is ETIQUETTE.

This is the way you play the game. Poor sportsmanship will make a negative impression and will give you an opportunity *not* to be invited back again — even if you win. If you lose a race with grace and honor, however, you'll be received with respect and open arms. As long as you give a sports audience plenty of excitement and enthusiasm (two of the main reasons people watch sports), they won't care whether you win or lose. They simply want to live the experience through you because, in most cases, they can't do it for themselves. They want to emulate a person of honor, and nobody likes a sore loser or an arrogant winner. With the proper etiquette, you don't have to be either one.

Etiquette is a higher level of thinking, a way of doing things that makes you and other people feel good — like apologizing when you're late, letting someone know you value their time and caring if you hurt somebody else's feelings. How long has it been since any of us even thought about etiquette, about holding grace and honor above winning a material prize? When everyone feels valued, your investment in a game, be it a sport or an aspect of daily life, will be richly rewarded.

CONSISTENCY is the third maxim.

This is a highly refined way to think about discipline. The burden of long-term, hard-core discipline eventually can break a person's nature and spirit. But when

nsistency is the result.

ut the external or the

resent with your kids,

narathon.

I could train and have

s my wife Jodi wanted

up together, she used

; when the alarm went

e only way to get me

commitment to what

o have her husband in

to know that if I began

ressed, climbed on the

sistency was about just

no clever reasons for

an get pretty elaborate!

on any given day. I just

ape, even though I felt

case, I owed it to Jodi

ich time and energy in

voiding conflict where

s an athlete, a husband

e training or even in a cycling race, it looks like second nature, doesn't it? She must be really enjoying herself or wouldn't it look harder? Most people can never conceive of the effort she's putting out or what came before—the time, the money, the training hours, the sleep deprivation, the nutritional management, the equipment, the pain and the dedication. This maxim is about making whatever you do shine. Although it usually doesn't show, a tremendous amount of effort in the face of adversity is involved in both training and in the race itself.

When an athlete learns to face adversity with maximum effort, there is a good chance to be victorious. On the other hand, the pampered athlete generally has little chance for accomplishment. If you complain about the headwind, the snow, the rain, the flat tire, the pain in your calves, while you dwell on how you nearly gave up and got off the bike, you're in trouble. All athletes must accept the fact that if you're not hurting, you're not going hard enough, but whether the output feels hard or easy is not the point. The point of the game is the mastery of self-confrontation. It's about continuing to press forward, to go with the flow of the energy and to be the best that you can be, no matter what the physical obstacles or the voices screaming in your head.

I have found that without exerting enough effort to go into the depths of what life has to offer, I'm not going to uncover the treasure within. Sure, we all keep on saying we want the house, the car, the happiness, the money, the trips, but these are by-products of effort in the face of adversity. The more effort we expend to dig into the nitty-gritty of the process, the more we participate, risk and accept pain, the freer we become.

SELF-CONTROL is the fifth and final maxim.

This is the key to harmonious accomplishment. It's really about following your instincts and knowing from the inside out that you have the power to do what it takes to accomplish your goals. When you can't maintain your breathing, when you lose your rhythm, your tempo and your timing, that's a loss of self-control. You have a sense of being in too deep and you can't pull out.

When you lose self-control, you also lose your ability to gauge your actions. This can result in fatal errors of consciousness. Political tyrants are examples of people with the fifth maxim out of balance, which causes them to see life in a state of nonreality. Using domination over someone with less power or treating employees like sexual objects are examples of loss of self-control. Balancing this maxim will help balance both mental and physical health and rid you of the delusions that will inevitably prevent you from realizing your dreams.

Before we leave this section on the intricacies of the relationship spoke, I must address sexuality, which is genetically coded into our structure. This is a tricky one, as our nature is to use sexuality for release—which is not about building a relationship in a dynamic, loving and harmonious way. In the past, I used sexuality as a way to reduce my personal frustration. You may know what I'm talking about—the kettle boils, you use someone else for release. When it's that base and simple, it can lead to prostitution, aggression and other forms of instant gratification that will eventually harm your soul and those of other people. The highest level for the fourth spoke is to honor sexual energy and use it to express love.

It's easy to know when the fourth spoke is off balance. Are you comfortable today with yourself and other people? If you're not, tweak the spoke, come back to yourself in integrity and get a little more conscious. Here, once again, all of the spokes demonstrate their connectedness. When you combine consciousness, good nutrition, healthy mind, emotions and thoughts with a good and honest relationship with yourself and others, you've got most of the qualities that it takes to make a champion—on the road, in the boxing ring, on the skating rink, in the playing field, in the kitchen or in the bedroom.

It's no longer beyond anyone's reach to be a realistic version of the White Knight who conquers life through cosmic awareness. I'm not referring to emotional or physical rescue. I'm talking about facing life with courage and inspiring that same courage in your friends and families. We can all work to erase negativity on the planet with cuts of intention toward awareness, power, integrity and character. We can all know the bliss of having the relationship spoke in balance, of being in harmony and of expressing a charismatic, dynamic personality.

The fourth spoke is a good road map for achieving personal power in all that you do. As with all the other spokes on the wheel, you need to be honest with yourself and stay open to the neighboring influences. Then you can move to the last spoke, that of realizing goals and dreams.

Seeding goals and dreams in my garden

GOALS AND DREAMS

THE FIFTH SPOKE is inexorably connected back to the first spoke, completing the circle of the wheel. If we agree that the structure of life starts with consciousness, then without goals and dreams we would lack the means to realize the most essential part of our being.

On July 29, 1979, when I was twenty-four years old, I got off a plane from South Africa, ready to take Los Angeles by storm. Although I'd always had my inner demons to fight, on the outside I'd lived a privileged life. My dad was a pharmacist and a champion athlete, we lived in a lovely neighborhood and we had three servants who catered to my every need. A cup of tea awaited me each morning no matter what time I woke up; all my clothes were washed by hand (somebody else's hand of course); I had an Alfa Romeo, a pretty girlfriend, a closet filled with expensive clothes and a good tan. In fact, I was taught that having a good tan and keeping my weight in line were the most important goals and dreams a young man could have. Needless to say, I had a few surprises in store.

My purpose (or so I believed at the time) for traveling to America was to stay for a month and learn about the gym business. The plan was that I would return to South Africa with my newfound knowledge and open a chain of successful gyms. I arrived feeling optimistic and I checked into the Pacific Sands Motel overlooking the beach. After a good night's sleep, I went to Gold's Gym to work out and to begin my research.

It was 10:00 A.M. when I returned to the motel. The sun was high and I was ecstatic to be in Los Angeles, confident that all was going as planned. I opened my motel room door to let in the light, grabbed a beach towel, some lotion and a good book to begin work on my tan, but it seemed that life had something else in store for me. Just as I was about to leave for the beach, an African American guy with a big Afro charged into my room, stuck a gun in my face and said, "Freeze, Motherfucker." In the instant he kicked the door closed behind both of us, my goals and dreams shifted. Suddenly, finding the best spot on the sand to put my towel, what I wanted for lunch, or how I wanted to perceive myself had lost all meaning. Now I wanted to live.

"Gimme some money," the gunman muttered as he inched closer to me, pointing the barrel straight at my head.

"I don't have any money," I told him. "I'm from South Africa, I just got here last night and we're not allowed to bring cash out of the country. But I've got three thousand dollars in traveler's checks. You can have them. I just have to sign them over to you."

He told me to lie down on the ground, stuck a pen in my hand, and with the gun at the back of my head I heard my mother's words from two days before. "Don't ever come back here," she'd said as I got on the plane. "You have everything you need. Go get your green card and make a real life for yourself where there are opportunities. Stay away from South Africa."

I lay on my belly, countersigning three thousand dollars worth of traveler's checks and giving them over, one by one, to this angry man who held my life in his hands. I figured he might as well shoot me because I wasn't going back home. On the other hand, I knew that twenty-four years old was too young to die. Thankfully, he left me with my life and a total of $6.10 in my pocket. Apparently he cashed the traveler's checks at the front desk of my own motel before he took off, while I stood in the shower where he'd ordered me to wait.

Three days later, gobbling up a frozen burrito I'd stolen from a Seven-Eleven convenience store, my dreams and goals didn't even slightly resemble what they were when I'd arrived in America. I had no intention of returning home, and somehow I knew I'd get through this and make it to the other side. It was time to realize the goals that my mother had dreamt for me while I was too scattered to dream them for myself. This was the beginning of putting the last of my spokes in order.

Goals and dreams, illusory as they may be, have helped me stay alive and kept the sun shining over my head during many a dark moment. Sometimes my dreams were all I had to keep me moving as I stepped over one obstacle after another to reach a finish line. During tough times when consciousness was elusive and I had no awareness of anything besides my pain, my goals and dreams offered me calmness, structure and perspective when I really needed them.

The fifth spoke combats the sense that life is mundane. If you think of the fifth spoke as the part of you that flowers like a rosebud when you put it in balance, it will begin to make sense. You'll start to see yourself not only as the caterpillar in gestation, but also as the realized butterfly, your daily training being the means to break free from the cocoon. First, though, in order to accomplish any goal you need a dream or a vision, and you need to do the continuing work of balancing your spokes.

If your relationships are sour, the pressure of your personal life could cause you to quit the game before you've reached your goal. It could even prevent you from joining the game at all. Maybe you're nutritionally undernourished, or your feelings and thoughts are racing out of control. Your consciousness snaps, spirituality dissolves and you're detached from the only thoughts that can keep you moving. Your life becomes a runaway train and you can no longer find your consciousness or awareness.

Several years ago when I became ill, I knew instinctively that I was one heartbeat away from not having the next one. One slipup in my breathing pattern would have meant the end of my life. My goals and dreams had been reduced to their base form: pure survival. As horrible as that was, it was also enlightening. I was experiencing the fifth spoke in its purest essence. My goal was to take another breath, my dream was to live. I understood at that time that breathing was not my right, it was my desire and my only goal. Each time I achieved it, the next breath immediately became my next goal. In this way, the fifth spoke had become my lifeline.

In an effort to keep the fifth spoke balanced, the tendency to step on people along the way can create a fickle and elusive journey. The connection of your goals and dreams to its adjacent spoke, that of relationships, is in question here. How do you maintain the proper etiquette and still keep your eye on the goal? Since intention drives your goals and dreams, you must make decisions whether to manifest them for good or for bad. This is where self-evaluation is crucial. How do you want to feel? What will bring you satisfaction? When the goal is to maintain balance among the spokes, you must look deeper than a simple desire to make a dream come true. You need to think about purpose, the needs of other people and identifying your place in life.

When dreams and goals become a person's obsession, when you choose to push your way over the very people you need to help you achieve that goal, you'll end up facing a myriad of problems: injuries, overtraining, drugs, steroids, anorexia, bulimia, dishonesty or depression. This is not only a trap for the athlete. When no price is too high to accomplish a particular goal, when no sacrifice is too much, when a human being cares nothing for another, the fifth spoke will be that person's downfall. There will be no structure, no happiness and no reason to get up in the morning. You may be antisocial, abusive, self-centered, overbearing, masochistic, sadistic, compassionless or any combination of the above. You get burned out, despondent; postpartum depression sets in after a race. When the fulfillment of a goal results in disappointment, spirituality has been lost and consciousness snaps off the wheel. By the way, if you think emotional imbalance is solely a female problem, that's not true. Emotions are nondiscriminatory and depression can bring the most macho of men to their knees.

With the fifth spoke out of balance, there is no longer a socialized sense of self. With no clarity or stability, what remains is a disoriented, confused individual, searching for answers with no trigger points along the way to serve as a reminder of what's real. This is when fanatical behavior takes over, as a good soldier becomes a Nazi, a fascist or a supremacist. This is when a heavyweight champion bites off his opponent's ear, a figure skater looks the other way when a member of her crew attacks her fellow skater, or a couple of angry kids shoot down their classmates and themselves in the library of their own school.

We all want purpose, not fear, to drive our desires and passions. At the end of our lives, we want to be able to rest in the knowledge that we lived according to what we wanted to do and who we wanted to be. At the same time we want to know that we were conscious, that we treated our loved ones with ultimate respect and that we did the same for ourselves. Accomplishing the impossible often takes more than we think we're capable of doing, and yet we manage. It may feel like you're so far off you'll never make it back, but I've seen that the human being sometimes needs to begin out of balance in order to find balance.

Back in 1979, after my money was stolen and I had no friends, I was aware that in order to realize my goals I needed other people. After staying up all night out of fear, walking the streets in Venice Beach with no bed and no food, I met a lovely couple who owned a veterinary clinic in Simi Valley. They offered me a job and I was grateful. My career as a veterinarian's assistant was short-lived, however, when I passed out from watching them perform a knee transplant on a Doberman Pinscher. It was back to the gym.

The "World for Men" health club was the most popular gym in Los Angeles at the time, where thousands of people worked out. Two employees there hired me at minimum wage ($3.25 an hour) to train people on the floor. While they went on vacation for two weeks I worked their shifts along with my own, waiting for my first paycheck while I slept on a drug dealer's floor, the only place I could find and a better option than the street. I ate free sugar cubes from the gym kitchen, I picked lemons, oranges and avocados that grew in the alleys in Santa Monica, and I accepted a couple of loaves of bread given to me on account by a convenience store merchant. In the meantime, I threw myself into my work at the health club, cleaning the exercise equipment, encouraging people, giving them massages and walking them to their cars when their workouts were over. I was so enthusiastic, I was so invested in helping people be the best they could be, my own dreams and goals were rubbing off on my clients. I thought I was on my way.

At the end of two weeks, I arrived at the gym excited to be picking up my first paycheck. The idea was to find an apartment and have a meal. Instead, the two employees who had hired me turned around and fired me, informing me that I had no green card so they owed me no money. They'd tricked me because their own dreams and goals were so pitifully out of balance. I was back out on the street with two additional problems: the drug dealer wanted to kill me because I had no money to give him for sleeping on his floor, and I couldn't pay back the convenience store merchant. This was a fork in the road. My dreams and goals would either lead me to my demise or become my salvation. It was difficult but I decided to stay calm; I continued to work out, and kept my focus on the road ahead.

The next day, Jim Shayne, the owner of World for Men, heard about what had happened because my clients were up in arms. They wanted me back. It turned out that with no prompting from me, Jim fired the two guys who had tricked me and hired me back for more money. He also signed my labor certification so I could work toward getting my green card and offered me the locker room in which to sleep until I had enough money to rent an apartment.

My story, although different from yours, may sound somewhat familiar to you. Everybody has their stories to tell and everybody goes through hard times. The task is to find a way to make your dreams come true—no matter what. You must strive to take heart in the face of adversity. You need to find a way to make the best of what you have, and not only accept your circumstances but go into them as deeply as you can. Then it becomes possible to achieve the most far-reaching dream without hurting anyone else.

If the athlete never actualizes a dream, if all your precious goals float off into Never Never Land, you'll never know the beauty of exploring and achieving your life's purpose. When you have the fifth spoke in balance, when you're focused on your dreams one hundred percent, upholding the commitment not to destroy anybody else in the wake of achieving your goals, you can accomplish the impossible. You can run the marathon, finish the cycling race or perform the toughest athletic event with all your heart. You can know the joy of participating in the game for the pure love and sport of it. You can wear your scars and blemishes like medals of honor, proof that you're keeping your wheel in balance while you take intelligent risks and pay the price that is yours to pay. In this way, athletes establish and fulfill their purpose.

The fifth spoke in balance can be blissful. When you look back at your life and see that it all made sense, that you were bold enough to dream and strong enough to achieve your goals along the way, you've identified your place in life. You've established who you really are, you've done what you were meant to do and you've become who you were meant to become. You've finished the RAAM, you've danced, you've raised a family, you've lost ten pounds, you've discovered a vaccine that saves lives, you've written a book, you've learned to walk again or maybe you've simply managed to take that necessary breath that will keep you alive. You are purely and completely YOU and you're proud of it.

Whatever the obstacles in your path, the essence of purpose doesn't change. The circumstances don't necessarily change either, but you do—into someone you can live with, someone you can love and someone who can love others. You've returned to consciousness, your life is in balance and the wheel keeps rolling.

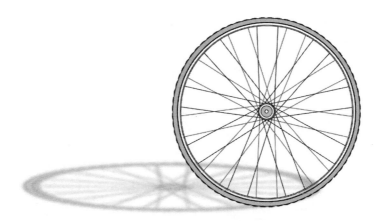

My students

THE SPINNING® PROGRAM

Since I created the Spinning program in the mid-eighties and presented it to the general public, I've been asked the same question almost every day of my life: What is Spinning? At first I was at a loss to describe this extraordinarily wonderful product, training program and insight that I had the honor and pleasure to birth and to grow. As the years have passed and millions of people have been exposed to the vision and experience of the Spinning philosophy, I've discovered an easier and more accessible way to think and talk about it.

My father once showed me a picture in a cycling magazine, which provided my inspiration for the name "Spinning." It was a photograph of a French cyclist crossing the Alps. His legs were bare, his tires were worn, his body was caked with mud, his lips were cracked and furrowed lines ran down both cheeks. The picture caught him in the process of making his dreams come true, stroke by stroke, breath by breath, spinning his web of commitment, as he made the hills and the pain disappear beneath him. Hence the name "Spinning" was born.

The meaning of Spinning is as simple as its name. The word describes a health and fitness program. It also describes a fun and easy way to learn an exercise philosophy that can work for anybody at any age. There are three basic hand positions and five basic body movements. Each session is taught by a certified Johnny G Spinning instructor at an authorized Spinning facility, in more than eighty countries around the world. To date, there are approximately forty thousand certified instructors who train up to fifty people in a single class.

The Spinning program consists of a forty-minute cardiovascular training performed on a specially designed stationary bike called the Johnny G Spinner.

73

I fashioned the bicycle so that participants could stand up and sit down in the saddle just like they can on a real road bicycle. I made sure it had no computer and therefore wouldn't recognize how many calories were being burned. That's because the Spinning program isn't about computers or burning calories. Although it has a strong physical component, the mental component is the cornerstone to the Spinning program.

I based the program on a philosophy that would level the playing field — no elimination of the weak for the strong, no qualifying, no fear of rejection, no competing with anyone but yourself. Since each participant is responsible for his or her own degree of exertion (a refreshing change after the last two decades in which the trainer ran the show), beginners and advanced students train side by side as individuals. And yet they still get the rewards of being in a pack, which includes the satisfaction of inspiring or being inspired by another person. While no one is brought down by anybody else's limitations, students can look to the side or in front of them and gain energy from people with higher levels of expertise.

In essence, the Spinning program is for any individual at any level of fitness who is willing to sit in the saddle, pedal and have a really good time listening to inspirational music, motivational language and insights about positive concepts, ideas and principles. The program offers a window of opportunity for everyone at all levels of fitness to know that, with perseverance, there is a place to grow and to become fit and strong.

Each session is designed to burn from four hundred to six hundred calories, the degree of energy output being ultimately left up to the participant. Since the training is highly intensive in nature, the use of a heart monitor allows the student to make an informed decision about the most beneficial level of exertion on any given day. With no impact on the joints or bones and no competition, the Spinning program marries physical, emotional and mental components. Years ago, this threefold integration was a budding concept without a name. Today we've come to know it as the mind/body connection, something I learned the hard way on the road.

I come from a realm of intensive outdoor athletic endeavor where the mind and the body must be in balance to achieve the ultimate goal. You see, I grew up believing that if I wasn't standing on the edge, I was taking up too much space. I didn't consider my limits because I couldn't find them. It's as if I was riding up a mountain with no respect or regard for the mountain, taking energy for granted, when eventually I stretched too far. Now I was in two disconnected pieces and the endeavor at hand became horrific. This kind of overtraining is not only a physical problem, it's also emotional, and it leaves mental scars that require tremendous fortitude, strength and mental discipline to heal. The Spinning program was designed as a structure that would offer a form of protection, a clarity and a sense of reading your own limitations, so you hit the off switch before the taffy gets stretched beyond its limit.

In my desire to avoid any further self-destruction, I've had to create principles and ways of acting and thinking that support me as a whole and happy human being. These principles were inbred into my consciousness through the RAAM, in which I participated twice. In creating the Spinning program, I used everything I got during my training for and participation in the RAAM. I faced adversity on every level, I was exposed to the extremes of pleasure and pain, directly experiencing the magic and majesty of life, and I learned about the nature of man through the stories of other human beings in the game. While I sweated blood and struggled with my torn-up flesh, the insufferable pain in my legs and the agony in my heart, I realized that we're all looking for the same things as we gather our pearls of wisdom along the way.

Some of these pearls are there for the taking, lying there right on the earth, shining up at us in clear sight. Other pearls are not so easy to obtain; they burrow deep beneath the surface and have to be dug out. Some of them are ugly, some are pretty, some are just barely manageable while others are liberating, but they are all necessary ingredients that make up the experiences of a balanced life. The true magic of a champion athlete is to use everything — every pearl and pedal stroke of pain and anguish, anxiety, frustration, disconnection, confusion, weakness and anything else that emerges along the way, good, bad or indifferent. This is the meaning of pure commitment.

After so many years of battling difficult terrain and unpredictable outdoor elements on the road, I took cycling indoors to create an opportunity for people who didn't want to ride a real bicycle. Even if you choose never to see the starting line of an actual race or deal with the winds, the deserts, the mountains and the leg cramps, I can still show you how to liberate yourself through the Spinning program. I can show you what it feels like to be in the middle or the front of the pack without suffering the humiliation of being dropped from the team because you aren't strong enough or skilled enough. You can close your eyes, listen to the music, get into a fluid rhythm and feel secure within the boundaries and parameters of your own experience. Whether you have weak knees, bad eyesight or only one leg, you can still embrace the techniques and

75

strategies that can make each and every person feel like a champion. You'll be able to say, "I can do this!" and you can know the glory and triumph of winning a race. Whatever is happening in your life, you can see that the bike will give you everything you need. It's as simple as that.

We live in a fast, demanding world, so we need to find a way to conserve energy or at least have the ability to replenish it. It's fine to run to the gym to pump up your biceps, to flatten your abs and to lose some weight. We all want great buns and we all want to be great lovers, but there are other ways to view health and fitness. We can ask ourselves the following questions: How do I feel right now? Am I strong and flexible? Are my legs dancing or do they feel sluggish? Am I congested? Do I feel restricted and limited or open and free? Do I feel powerful enough to complete the task that lies ahead of me? Is my drive for exercise based on looking good enough to take off my shirt or am I interested in feeling fit, strong and healthy?

Since the outside reflects the inside and the body follows the mind, your desire to go deeper, to be grounded and to be emotionally balanced will reflect outward in every aspect of your life. When you train yourself to sit quietly and to take pride in mundane activities like doing your laundry or working in the garden, you're opening your heart to the core issues of life. That's when you start to eat, think and even breathe differently.

The Spinning program exists today to show people how to nurture themselves as they train their bodies and their minds without guilt, without feeling responsible to anyone but themselves and without pushing beyond their abilities until the mind gives way. In a forty-minute training session, I want to help people find a sweet rhythm in an otherwise unforgiving world, a peace and a comforting sense of solitude in which they can drop anxiety from their heads and hearts. I want to take anyone who thinks they don't measure up and settle them into the pack where they can find their own natural rhythm. Together, I want us all to plant seeds that will blossom into beauty and inspiration. True, we're all dropping sweat onto the floor. True, we all hear the screech of the bike and feel the burn of the muscles. But we also understand that with each droplet of energy exerted and each muscle burn, we are building ourselves a living structure of growth, strength and abundance. That's another pearl that I got on the road:

Giving everything you have will automatically give you back exactly what you need.

The Spinning program was designed to show you that the stationary bike, potentially the most boring piece of equipment imaginable, can be brought to life, but only if you have a true urge to imbue it with energy. The simple act of pedaling is not enough to create such a purpose. Neither are the acts of sweating, burning calories or losing weight. The Spinning program is much more all-inclusive. It's about surrendering to the Universe, freeing the mind, opening the heart and creating personal parameters. It's about building a structure and a plan to get somewhere—while you're standing still, pedaling and going nowhere. Finally, its about liberating every cell as you ride the bike with inspiration and direction, even if your intention is as simple as pedaling for ten minutes to the next mountain. Big or small, that mountain can be anything you want it to be. Whether your goal is to win a race, heal an illness, make peace with your emotions or just get through a difficult day with an open heart, this program is there to help you achieve that goal.

As time has passed, I've seen stationary cycling take on a life of its own. I've seen it spawn indoor cycling competitors and new facsimiles of stationary bicycles. I've watched it encompass sex appeal, music, rhythm, timing, breathing, pizzazz and the finesse of feeling like a superstar champion. I've had the opportunity to witness a simple concept called "Spinning" explode into a revolution in the way people think about training without the unnecessary bells and whistles. Most importantly, I've watched stationary cycling give people an opportunity to express their individuality. When they feel the urge, they can stand up out of the saddle, close their eyes, feel the rhythm of the music, and let themselves go. And when they need the time to back off and regain energy, they can do that too, without feeling guilty.

Whether you're an athlete, a businessman, or suffering from a degenerative disease, whether Spinning is a consistent part of your life or you use it to drive you to future goals or dreams, the gift of the Spinning program can be synthesized into one vital message:

You are the most important person in the world. Never stop believing in yourself. No matter what it takes, get out there and keep it simple. Be respectful, be aware, be conscious and develop a mentality that will allow you to give yourself a good shot at a rewarding life. You deserve it.

My life today

THE FINAL STAGE

As this book draws to a close, the preceding pages turn out to be the end result of all that came before: the synthesis of a life. And yet with life, there is never an ending. There are only transitions to the next levels of existence, however different they may look for each of us.

The writing of this book has been a fascinating journey for both Andrea and me. As simple as we intended for it to be, it has spanned two millenniums, several years of creative meetings, countless philosophical discussions, in-depth psychological archeology, a bout with the throes of life and death and, eventually, a serious search for sanity. Nothing ever unfolds the way we expect.

Although we have our individual paths to follow as we complete our allotted days here on earth, there are certain inexorable dreams and goals that all human beings share. We want happiness, satisfaction, fulfillment and a mental and physical vitality that makes us glad to be alive. In a spiritual sense, we want consciousness and awareness, a sound mind and an open heart. In short, we want life to be more than simply getting through the day; we want something we can count on. We want to look good, feel good about ourselves and others and most of all, we want our lives to have meaning. When we look back at the end of our time here, we need to know in our heart of hearts that we lived well, we learned as much as we could and we offered something valuable and precious to the next generation.

When I was recovering from my debilitating illness, I went to a martial arts camp to train with a high level *sensai* in the Japanese art of Boh Jitsu. I chose this specialized training for its qualities of introspection, fluidity of movement and the opportunity to isolate and break down individual body parts into their simplest form in synchronicity with a wooden staff.

In preparation for the camp, I'd spent many months with a piece of sandpaper, transforming a six-foot-long wooden block with sharp edges into a perfectly rounded thinner staff called a *boh*. As I poured love and energy into my work, I got fit and strong while I watched the grains of sand falling off my staff. When I finally held the fruit of my labor in my hand, I understood that I could never bring back the grains that had fallen to the ground. They were gone forever as my life would be one day, and I sincerely wanted it to be remembered as something of value.

At 4:30 in the morning, when the master and I stood in an open clearing on his Arizona retreat, I had my stick outstretched from the center of my body, pointed upwards at a forty-five degree angle. As the morning light began to cast an ethereal glow on the surrounding cacti and fragrant eucalyptus trees, I spotted a dove peacefully flying across the open area in which we stood. Suddenly his claws hit the tip of my staff where he perched for an instant, sending vibrations throughout my body. The master, hearing the sound of claws slipping on the wood, watched as the bird lit momentarily and then flew away. Together we had witnessed the harmony of man and nature—the true magic of life.

The dove had broken the morning silence, demonstrating to me that the real magic of life was not about the ruthless practice of putting energy out and abusing my body so I could win a race. I'd done that my whole life, pumping iron, riding on metal, until I'd collapsed—disappointed, debilitated and empty of heart and mind. Rather, the beauty of my life today was about taking energy in, building strength from the inside out, thereby renewing myself into a harmonious, life-affirming existence.

I am happy to say that at this moment in time I am restored to a complete state of health, my brain is clear, my heart is healthy, my body is strong and so is my mind. In a recent discussion with Andrea concerning my illness, I referred to it as "the time I got sick." She suggested that I'd been sick for a long time, and the episode that brought me down was, in essence, the time that I began to get well.

I wholeheartedly agree with her. The period in which I fought for my life forced me to throw out all my outdated, narrow-minded beliefs and philosophies and to reconstruct a new and healthy structure with the Five Spokes of Balance at the foundation. As a result, Johnny G and Jonathan Goldberg finally have become equal parts of an integrated whole, representing an athlete with compassion, the kind of human being I can respect and love.

As I close this book, I'm proud to say that I'm back and I'm working to keep my heart open. I'm ready to take on the next phase of my life with deep gratitude, tremendous hope and a hard-earned ability to see beyond myself and into the hearts and needs of others.

When a human being uses his physical power to lash out at someone, he is not only destroying the other person, he is also destroying himself. When he builds his inner awareness and shines it outward on someone, he is not only nurturing his friend, he is also nurturing himself. As we each work to build our own inner strength, to heal the past and be present in the moment, we are awakening our consciousness and awareness. We are building our dreams and goals for a beautiful future as we free ourselves to accept all that life has to offer, right here, right now.

This book is my offering, my truth in each moment, my pearls of wisdom that I've gathered from direct experience. Please accept it in the spirit in which I give it, allowing my stories of personal pain and pleasure to connect you to your own. Life is filled with so many possibilities. As we all search to accomplish our goals and dreams, I wish you a healthy body, clarity of mind and the consciousness to know when to push forward and when to pull back. It's all about finding a balance between energy in and energy out, and the wisdom to know the difference.

When I lived in South Africa, my buddy from a gang called the "Preston Bum Rushes" used to say:

Don't rat-a-tat-tat on my head, don't jive on my concert, don't zigzag all over me like a crab.

In America, my cycling buddies say:

Keep the rubber side down and a smile on your face.

In plain English, they both mean:

Take good care of yourself and allow your life to reflect right perception, discovery and awareness.

Please remember these simple guidelines:

When in doubt, seek the guidance of a professional to help you stay focused on your goals and dreams. There is no right or wrong way to live your life, so don't try to give what you don't have. Just figure out what you really want and point your bicycle in the direction of your intention. If you strive to do this from a place of right intention and honesty, if you care enough about your loved ones and yourself to make wise decisions for all involved, that's a life well-lived.

And it's enough.